How to pay for the Wedding you *really* want

D. L. Chikwendu

A publication by Purple Panel Limited

Published by Purple Panel Limited (First Revised Edition)
Copyright © D. L. Chikwendu 2009

A CIP catalogue record for this book is available from the British Library

Purple Panel Limited
PO Box 1032
Enfield
London
EN1 9EW

ISBN 978-0-9564176-0-2

www.purplepanel.co.uk/publications.aspx

All rights reserved. No part of this publication may be reproduced, stored in a retrieval system, or transmitted, in any form or by any means, electronic, mechanical, photocopying, recording or otherwise, without the prior permission of the copyright owner.

Contents

Introduction	Page 4
Chapter 1: The big question - What sort of wedding do you *really* want?	Page 7
Chapter 2: What you will need to get started	Page 16
Chapter 3: What will you need to create the income?	Page 28
Chapter 4: Creating your 1st online income stream	Page 38
Chapter 5: Creating auction links and more to add to your website	Page 53
Chapter 6: How to advertise the products and services you want to promote	Page 75
Chapter 7: Using Amazon to make money by promoting products	Page 90
Chapter 8: Using APPs to generate the income you want	Page 109
Chapter 9: How much income can you make to pay for the wedding you *really* want	Page 130
Wedding resources that you may find helpful for your special day	Page 140
About the Author	Page 141
Acknowledgments	Page 142

Introduction

In reality ladies (and gentlemen) we are not all born into the Billionaires' club, so paying for the wedding of our dreams becomes a challenge that may seem more overwhelming than we initially thought. These days, supermarkets, high street banks and glossy magazines lure us towards their solutions of applying for loans to fund our dream weddings and if possible, if we can imitate a diluted version of our favourite celebrity wedding, then the better we will appear to be to everyone around us (apparently).

Wedding days are supposed to be deeply special occasions and are often a time for families and friends to enjoy a union of celebration and happiness. Of course, the day is ultimately about the beautiful union between a couple and in an ideal world, who wants to keep thinking about what else is left to pay off on a balance for a wedding of a lifetime?

I got happily married in July 2008 and even though my husband and I had a lovely day, in the back of my mind as the day drew to an awesome close that dreaded question popped into my head, "How much and how long will it take for us to pay this off?"

I did all that I could to reduce the cost of the wedding day for my husband and I, I even project-managed the day myself and handed over the itinerary for the day to my Mistress of Ceremonies (my gorgeous sister), but post-wedding there were still minor items that had to be paid for, not to mention our honeymoon to the Maldives...

Prior to my wedding, I did my research regarding paying for a wedding but often stumbled across other pieces of advice such as focusing on the countdown plan (i.e. what key tasks to do each month like deciding on a date, booking the venue, etc) or the top ten things that must be included in the "perfect wedding" which suggested wearing a Vera Wang wedding dress – at least! The main options that I found from my research at the time regarding how to pay for a wedding, can be summarised in five main options:

- How to plan a wedding on a shoestring budget - not quite the type of wedding we were looking for.

- How a wedding can be paid for from your savings – but what if you do not have much?

- How a wedding can be paid for via a bank or building society loan – oh no, yet more debt.

- How Parents or family members (even friends) can sponsor the day – this is great but then you are likely to inherit a team of six wannabe wedding planners telling you what flowers you should have or how many guests should attend - who cannot include Aunt Joan because Mum is not talking to her...

- How to use credit cards to pay for the wedding - another loan/credit agreement to pay off over the next ten years...no thanks.

There was no advice out there suggesting ways of generating income to pay for the wedding of your dreams WITHOUT having to get into more debt, emotional obligation or having to get involved in family politics.

My husband and I ended up combining the above options i.e. our parents contributed what they could, we used some of our savings, but the majority of the wedding was funded by a loan which (may I add) we are still paying back!

This may not be a glossy magazine or advice from the best wedding book in the world, but I can assure you that it will open up your mind to the possibility of creating a number of ways to generate alternative income that has nothing to do with your regular day (or night) job.

This book is written to provide information about how you (and your partner) can utilise the internet so that you can generate and build up a healthy bank balance to supplement (or create) savings for the wedding that you *really* want. If I knew this information at least six months to a year before getting married or at the time of getting engaged, my introduction would have been a showcase of the dream wedding I *really* wanted and managed to have! Well guess what? YOUR DREAM WEDDING IS POSSIBLE and you can have all the things or events that will make your day special. The sky's the limit!

Heads-up!

This book offers a combination of tasks and actions, tips and references. The information in this book offers suggestions only and it is the sincere intention that this will help you and your partner to have the wedding that you *really* want and hopefully it will help you both to avoid settling for anything less than what you *really* want for your special day. This is not about the size of the wedding or the number of guests, but rather the focus is to be able to pay for the quality that you have dreamed of.

The guidance offered in this book feature methods that are legitimate, however whatever you choose to do as a result of reading and following the steps in this book, please ensure that your actions comply with any ethical, local, national and international requirements. Do not use these methods to exploit or deceive others.

So who is this book for?

It is with sincere intention that no matter what your background is, you will find the information in this book useful and of interest somehow. The main thing that is needed to create and move forward with anything is to take POSITIVE ACTION. Often the difference between getting what you *really* want and settling for whatever you can get, depends on whether or not you want to take any ACTION.

Whether you have a Sugar Daddy (or Mama) or even a well to do spouse-to-be, I hope that you find the information in this book helpful in supporting you to get the wedding that you *really* want.

I strongly suggest that you read through this book once and then read it again to register the information contained. Then TAKE POSITION ACTION, STEP BY STEP.

Here we go!

Chapter 1 - The big question: What sort of wedding do you *really* want?

For the majority of couples who want to make the ultimate commitment via marriage (or civil partnership), the first question is usually based along the lines of "So when should we get married?" Imagine if all you had to really focus on was clarifying what your ideal wedding would be and that money was in fact a background question.

There are many ways that assist couples in subsidising the financial burden. Glossy lifestyle magazines, TV shows and reputable websites offer seasonal competitions where the grand prize can include the full or partial payment for the wedding of your dreams. These can also include covering the cost of a honeymoon of a lifetime. This can be one way of paying for the wedding you *really* want, but unfortunately there is no guarantee.

So back to the question – what sort of wedding do you *really* want?

How to visualise the wedding you *really* want

Traditionally, weddings tend to target the ladies because ever since she can remember it has likely to have been something that she has imagined. Light years ahead of the day, she has already visualised the ideal dress, the most romantic venue on earth and the perfect honeymoon destination. The men (or significant others) on the other hand tend to be left out of the loop and traditionally have not always been asked what would make an ideal wedding to them. LADIES, it is important to include your partner-to-be in regards to the type of wedding you want and men – likewise.

STEP 1 - Have an honest and open discussion with your partner about what you both want

This is no ordinary discussion. Remember the focus is detailing the type of wedding you *really* want – so do not hold anything back! The purpose of this discussion is to extract all the exciting and creative things that you believe would make your wedding special to both of you.

STEP 2 - Create a mind map diagram

TASK - Get a piece of paper (the larger the better) and a pen and create a similar diagram to the one below. Spend as long as you can and write down all the things that would be included in the wedding of your dreams. See the example below:

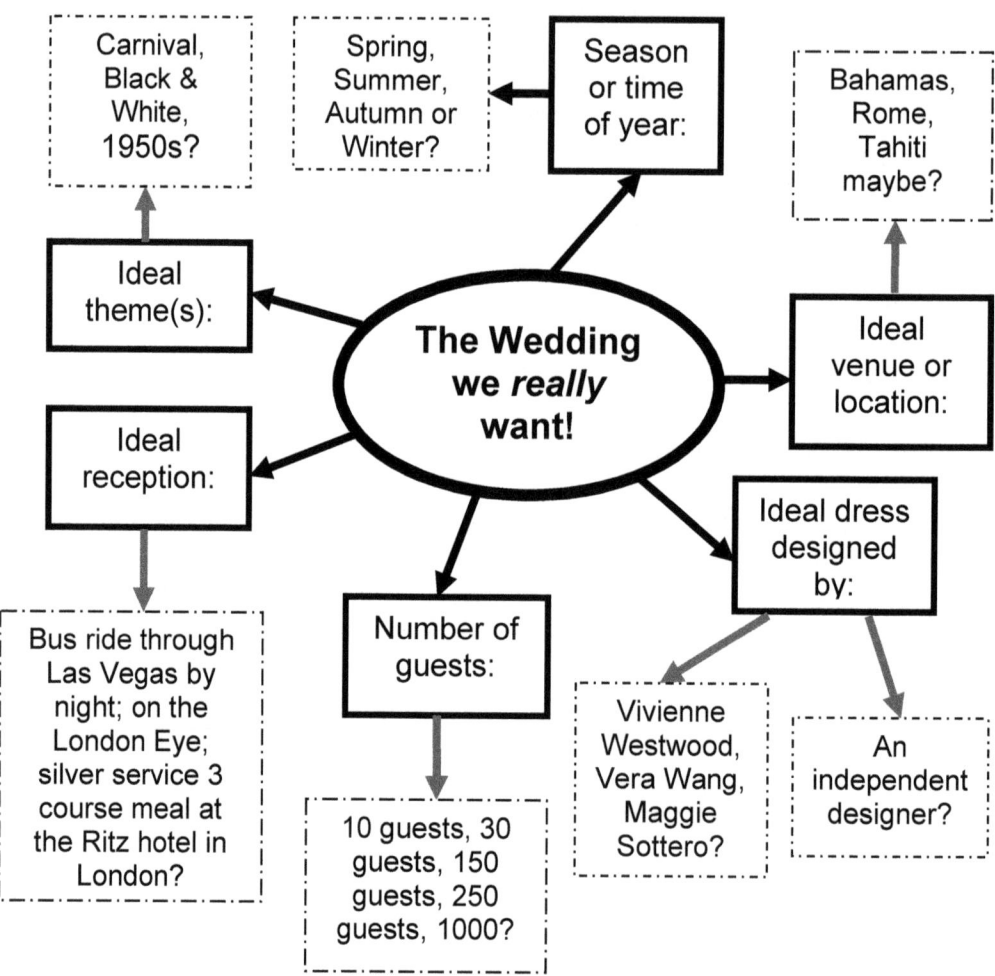

TIP – You may want yourself and your partner to do this activity separately. Then after you have both written down your individual desires, come together and compare your ideas. Your ideas can be as unusual as you want. Remember this is about having the wedding you *really* want, not limited by the kind of wedding you can *afford* – there is a BIG difference.

STEP 3 - Combine your ideas

After combining your ideas regarding the type of wedding you *really* want, decide and agree on items or activities you MUST have or do everything! REMEMBER – you can have the wedding you *really* want. DO NOT let logic get in the way. The purpose of the activity is not to create an argument. This is supposed to be fun! You may try to talk yourself out of it, so push away your thoughts of being sensible for once – what do you *really* want?

STEP 4 - The fun part!

After deciding with your partner what features must be a part of the wedding that you *really* want, create a visual storyboard of your wedding. There are two main ways you can create this:

Hardcopy storyboard (Getting your hands dirty/ practical)	Digital storyboard (Keeping your hands clean)!
This can involve buying magazines, newspapers, sourcing images from the internet, cutting these out and sticking them onto a piece of card of your choice. The larger the card the better because the purpose behind creating this is so that it can hang in a place where both you and your partner can refer to it. Alternatively, you could source pictures or photos that summarise your ideal wedding and frame or stick these to a wall of your choice. The benefit of this method is that it can be more accessible than storing a digital storyboard on your laptop or computer, i.e. you	This can involve using the internet as your main source for searching for images. For example, you can use online functions like Google Images or visiting photo resource centres – when you do a Google or Yahoo search, type in "free stock photos" to review a range of websites that offer free photos. Rather than printing and cutting up these images and sticking them to a board or a large piece of card, you can create a digital slide show using Microsoft PowerPoint. Even though this can be less accessible, this can be easily emailed to yourself and your partner and in theory (if you have

| would have to switch on your computer then open your saved file to view this. | the time) you can remind yourselves of the wedding you *really* want by viewing this slide show or showing colleagues/ friends during breaks at work. |

The core purpose of creating a visual storyboard of the wedding that you *really* want is so that you can remain motivated. You can *see* or visualise the desired outcome. An example of some storyboards follow:

Lisa and Dave's Ideal Wedding – December, year 20_____			
Wedding Location: St Lucia, Caribbean	Lisa's dress	Dave's suit	Wedding bands by Hamiltons, Hatton Garden, London
Gift List: Tiffany & Co	Flowers by Preston Bailey	Possible Bridal Accessories	Cake by Paul – Maison de Qualité, fondée en 1889

Rina and Kai's Ideal Wedding – June, year 20_____			

Wedding Location: Las Vegas	Number of guests: 2	Reception: Private dinner for 2 at the Bellagio Hotel	Wedding bands by Tiffany & Co

Sarah and Femi's Ideal Wedding – May, year 20_____		

Wedding Location: the Ritz Hotel, London	Sarah's dress	Theme: Church wedding, Gold and Ivory

STEP 5 - Defining the cost of the wedding you *really* want

Now that you have created a clear vision of what you want your wedding to look like you have to work out how much it will cost.

TASK – For every area of your wedding find out quotes or estimates of how much each element of your dream wedding will cost. Be sure to use your storyboard as a point of reference and decide how long you want to take to achieve your financial goal. Let's use the example of Rina and Kai's wedding storyboard.

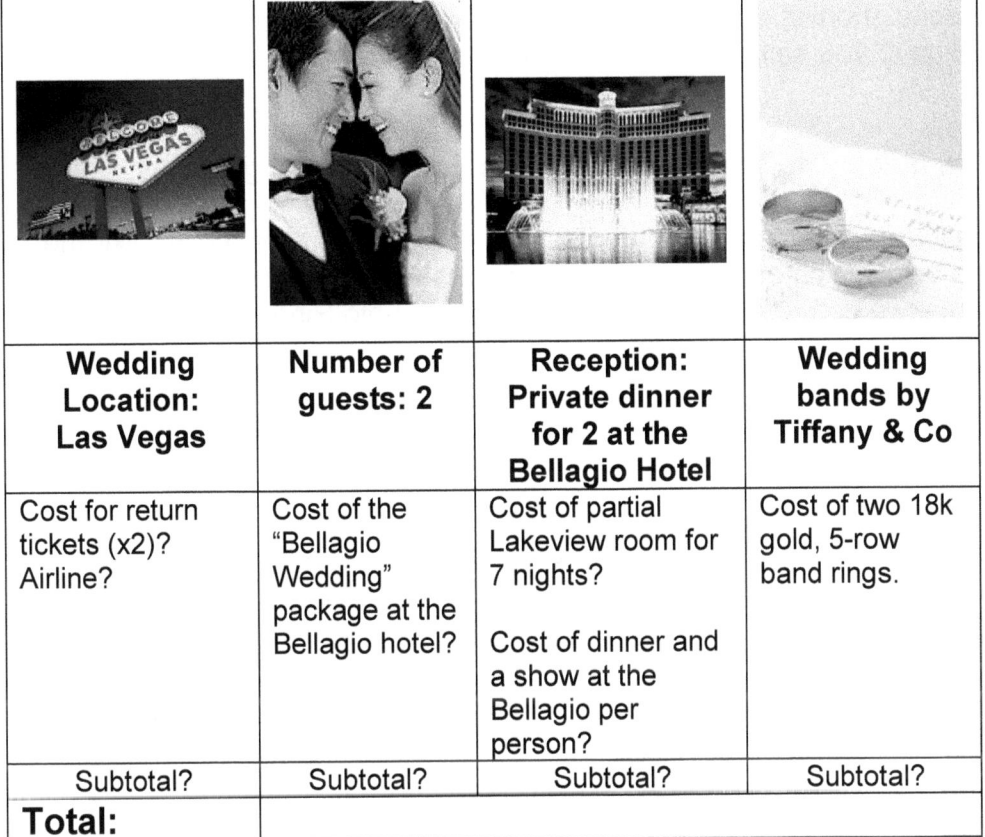

Wedding Location: Las Vegas	Number of guests: 2	Reception: Private dinner for 2 at the Bellagio Hotel	Wedding bands by Tiffany & Co
Cost for return tickets (x2)? Airline?	Cost of the "Bellagio Wedding" package at the Bellagio hotel?	Cost of partial Lakeview room for 7 nights? Cost of dinner and a show at the Bellagio per person?	Cost of two 18k gold, 5-row band rings.
Subtotal?	Subtotal?	Subtotal?	Subtotal?
Total:			

TIP – Be sure to take a note of all the sources of your quotes to save you time later. You do not want to be in a position of trying to remember what website you visited to get a great flight deal to your dream destination!

TIP – Attempt to set yourself a limited time to achieve or gain certain quotes or overall goals to deliver something. The purpose of this research is so that you get an estimate of what your financial target is. Add 1.3% to the total financial target of the wedding that you really want (this represents a buffer amount in case of any unplanned expenses or fees).

Also when you create a limited time period, you are forced to be more productive and to only focus on tasks that will give you the desired results or quotes that you want. For example, if you set yourself one evening to research quotes for flights to Las Vegas, you are more likely to only select a shortlist of websites or companies to contact in comparison to if you gave yourself one week – you would waste too much time!

How quickly do you want to achieve your financial goal?

After you have located the quotes that you need, create a chart like the one below. You and your partner can then set a time to achieve this goal. Again, we can refer to the example of our couple Rina and Kai:

Rina and Kai's Ideal Wedding – June, year 20_____			
Wedding Location: Las Vegas	**Number of guests: 2**	**Reception: Private dinner for 2 at the Bellagio Hotel**	**Wedding bands by Tiffany & Co**
Cost for return tickets (x2): £1670.00* travelling with Virgin Atlantic	Cost of the "Bellagio Wedding" package at the Bellagio: £2560.00*	Cost of partial Lakeview room for 7 nights: £1284.00* Cost of dinner and a show at the Bellagio per person: £145.70*	18k gold, 5-row band ring, £485* per ring.
£1670.00	£2560.00	£1429.70	£970
Total:	**£6629.70**		

14

Sources:	*http://www.virginatlantic.co.uk , http://www.bellagio.com and http://uk.tiffany.com (All quotes were correct at the time of sourcing this information).

In total, the cost of the wedding that Rina and Kai really want is £6629.70. Rina and Kai have decided that they want to generate enough finance at least 1 year before they actually get married. Rina suggests that they *aim* to generate this amount within a 6 month time frame; allowing time for any changes.

First of all they multiple the total cost of their wedding by 1.3% to include any unplanned expenses: £6629.70 x 1.3% = **£8618.61**

TASK – Since you and your partner have already calculated how much the wedding you *really* want will cost, multiple the total by 1.3%. **This total is your target income.** Type your target into a Microsoft Word document and enlarge it enough to catch your attention. Title this page as "Our target income." Next add this sentence:

1) Our monthly target income = £ _____ (divide your target by 12 if your time frame is 12 months).

TIP – To make your financial target clearer, divide your monthly target by 30 (average number of days in a month). Add a sentence to your Word document that states:

2) Our daily target income = £ _____ . For example, if we use the example of our couple Rina and Kai:

Rina and Kai's Total income target = £8618.61
Monthly Target Income = £8618.61 / by 6 (i.e. 6 months) = £1436.44
Daily Target Income = £1436.44/ by 30 (i.e. 30 days) = £47.90

£47.90 is Rina and Kai's daily income target.

PRINT AND POST YOUR MONTHLY AND DAILY TARGET INCOMES IN A PLACE THAT YOU CAN BOTH SEE THEM EACH DAY. THIS IS IMPORTANT TO HELP YOU STAY FOCUSED.

With all of this done, you are ready to move forward – let's go!

Chapter 2 – What you will need to get started

To re-cap from the previous chapter, so far you have:

- Had several discussions with your partner about the wedding you both *really* want.

- Created a visual storyboard purposed as a prompt and motivational tool.

- Sourced realistic quotes regarding how much the wedding you *really* want will cost.

- Defined what your monthly and daily income targets are so that you can have the wedding that you *really* want.

So what will you need to generate income to have the wedding that you *really* want?

The essential criteria can be divided into two groups:

Non-tangible	Tangible
Your time As a suggestion, decide to allocate at least 2 – 3 hours a day to work through these steps. This can be done alongside a day job, but you must re-prioritise your time.	A copy of this step by step guide
Motivation This will keep you moving towards your goal to have the wedding that you *really* want	Internet access and a computer or laptop that enables internet access
Patience This is essential – this is likely to be a new process of knowledge and information. There are no magic formulas of "quick-fix" strategies, so be patient and work through each step.	A bank account for depositing your income including a bank or credit card (to invest approximately £50 - £100 initially depending on what you choose to do)

Focus The purpose of completing certain tasks and steps supports you in staying focused.	A PayPal account from https://www.paypal.com/uk/
Determination If you believe you can have the wedding that you really want, then stay determined to make it a reality.	An A4 note pad to record your activity and ideas (remember to date all that you input into this dedicated place)

TIP – With a full time job and responsibilities it may seem impossible to be able to allocate any of your social or evening time to a mini-project like this, however when was the last time you were able to pay for something (or an experience) that you wanted by watching a number of TV shows one after the other?

As a suggestion, review what you would normally watch on TV and how much time you would spend on the internet browsing without any specific purpose. Decide what shows or activities you must watch (or do) and eliminate the rest. Instead allocate the remainder of the time in dedication to following the steps of this guide to generate income to have the wedding you *really* want.

Do you have all that you need to get started?

The items in the left hand column of the table are qualities that you will gain along the way and even if you have these already, it is good to be able to build and strengthen these qualities.

In the instance where gaining the items you need in the right hand column of the table, this may be completely new to you, so a quick guide follows. On the bright side, you already own a copy of this step by step guide to support you.

Purchasing a computer or laptop with internet access

In this age, most people have access to a computer or laptop. To generate online income, you may want to consider the following suggestions:

1) **Have access to a personal computer or laptop from your home - RECOMMENDED**

There are advantages and disadvantages to this option including:

Advantages	Disadvantages
• **Flexibility** – you can access the internet whenever you need to for any length of time you choose.	• The comfort of your own home can be ideal, but its environment can also offer day to day distractions. You can overcome this by allocating a certain space and time to dedicate your efforts towards your goal.
• **Privacy** - you can work on generating your automated income without someone peeping over your shoulder.	• Initially, it will feel as if you are leaving your regular day (or night) job only to start another. Attempt to revise the way that you see your activities. Remember this is so you can get the wedding that you *really* want!
• There is no "start-up" cost to having this access if you already have a computer or laptop with internet access/ wireless capabilities.	• Continuing your usual routine can cause you to sometimes waste your time without realising it. Draft a new routine for yourself and do it!

2) Have access to a laptop from a local cyber cafe, pub or Net bar

Advantages	Disadvantages
• **Cost effective** – If you are unable to invest or spend the money on a computer or laptop, this option could meet your needs for the time being.	• **Time is limited** – depending on the type of work you do to earn money, you will have to locate an internet cafe that is convenient and affordable.
• **Can create greater focus** - Working in this type of	• **Lack of privacy** – unlike being in the comfort of your

environment can cause you to focus more and to be decisive about what you are going to achieve in the time. For example, if all you can afford is to stay for 1 hour – what are your priority tasks?	own home, there is always the possibility of people showing unwanted interest in what you are doing.

TIP – Libraries, local community centres and schools or academies often offer free internet access or services so it may be worth finding out from your Local Authority or Council what services are available.

I do not recommend using the computers and free broadband at your place of work for this type of project/ activity. It is best to keep this separate from your work or job.

Purchasing a computer or laptop

To purchase a computer there are a number of places that you can purchase Net books (mini laptops), standard laptops and computers. Here are a few suggestions:

- www.dell.com
- www.pcworld.com OR www.pcworld.co.uk
- http://www.apple.com/uk/
- www.hp.com.uk

TIP - There are likely to be a number of retailers and online stores that allow you to purchase laptops and computers. Be sure that they are reputable retailers. If in doubt, you can always ask for recommendations from family and friends or work colleagues.

Internet access options

There are a number of ways that you can gain access to the internet, but the two main methods for home or personal use are likely to include the following:

- **Mobile** – Most mobile phone or telecommunications companies have mobile broadband available via a pen or USB memory stick. Some networks offer a "pay as you go" tariff or you can pay for mobile internet access via a monthly contract.

- **Subscription** - Subscribing to the Internet as a part of a package with a Cable TV or digital TV company such as Virgin Media, Sky etc. There are a number of companies that offer internet services. You may want to use comparison websites to ensure that you are getting value for money. As a suggestion, type in "Internet service providers" into Google at www.google.co.uk or www.google.com.

Having a bank account and a bank or credit card

If you are currently employed or have worked you are likely to already have the above facilities. It will be your choice to use your day to day bank account, but it may not be the best way forward. You may want to keep salary and/ or wages separate from your mini project or maybe you have concerns about using your main account for online activities. If so, you may want to consider the following options:

- **Use a "forgotten" account** - Use an account that you do not use for your day to day transactions. For example, you may have a past student account or a current account that you use for gifts or as a back-up account for whatever reason. Current accounts usually have a bank card connected to the account that you can use.

- **Open a new account** - If you have a good name in the business world (i.e. you manage your finances well and have not likely to defaulted any type of payments required from you), then open a new account that you can use specifically for this activity or project. This way you can keep a separate track of what goes in and out of your account (the basic principle of cash flow) without confusing it with your day to day bill payments, salary etc.

In regards to a credit card, depending on who you bank with, you may already have a credit card. Hopefully, this will have a low balance or none at all which is even better!

But what if you do not have a credit card?

As a suggestion, you may want to consider the following options:

- **Are you a safe bet?** It is important to know how you are perceived in the business world, i.e. are you a candidate that the banks would lend credit or loans to? You can know this by taking an interest of finding out what your credit rating or score is. Go online and visit http://www.creditexpert.co.uk . You can sign-up for a free trial and report, but be prepared to pay a small fee to know what your credit score is.

Once you know what your rating or score is you can have more confidence when applying for a credit card if you do not have one. Of course, this is not a guarantee, since some companies will have their own lending criteria.

- **Find out what credit cards are available** - There are a number of companies to approach when applying for a credit card, but as a starting point ask the institution that you bank with to offer guidance. Also be sure to be clear about the interest rates and what is expected from you. As a suggestion, I do not recommend that you use this credit card to supplement your day to day living. This should be used in relation to generating online income only.

Creating a Pay Pal account

It is important to be able to receive payments online and for that to happen a Pay Pal account is required.

Pay Pal is a service that offers individuals and companies the ability to be able to conduct online transactions **securely**. Customers can pay for goods securely using their credit or debit cards. Products and services can also be paid for via email. Once an account is open, a range of options can be utilised like creating buttons for online stores or purchases.

If you are not familiar with Pay Pal, you may find it helpful to visit - www.paypal-business.co.uk .

But before I offer brief guidance about how to create a Pay Pal account, it is important to consider whether or not you would like to operate online as an individual or to operate under a company name.

For example, I operate under Purple Panel Ltd. You can view the website at www.purplepanel.co.uk . Even though I have registered this as an actual company, with a registered trademark, PO Box address and business banking accounting, you do not have to go through this level of registration. HOWEVER, after you have read this book once or twice and registered the information contained and what action needs to be considered and done, you may decide to create a similar set-up.

You can do this at a later time, but if you want to "test" operating online as an individual, then I strongly recommend that you to consider the following:

- **Think of a name to operate under that sounds professional –** For example if your name is Claudia Cousins, avoid calling your trading name this. Think of a name that could be used in the longer term or which could sound like a company or a name that you would trade under if you were self-employed. The purpose is not to deceive others but to protect your personal information in the same way that you would create a personal email account, i.e. it is usually a manipulation of your real name or significant details.

- **Think about purchasing or renting a PO Box address –** I strongly recommend that you avoid using your personal home address and find out how you could have your own PO Box address.

    Visit http://www.royalmail.com/portal/rm and type in "PO" into the search box:

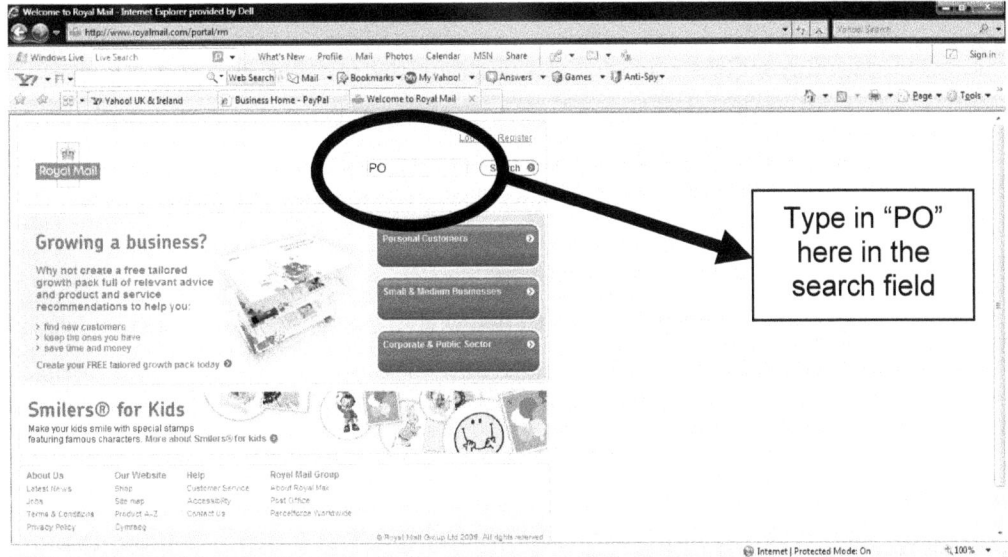

- A page showing the list of your search results will include "PO Boxes®" click on this link to find out more information about setting this up. Once set up, you can instruct Royal Mail to re-direct any post sent to your PO Box to be delivered to your home address for your convenience.

- **Register an email address** – I strongly recommend that you register a specific email address to manage all your contact and online activities. If you have an existing email address, you may consider using this for the meantime, but please note that if you use this for personal contact to communicate with family and friends etc; you may not want to confuse activities outside of this.

- **Allocate a mobile number to your operating name** – The development of technology and communications have driven us towards being able to communicate at our convenience from almost anywhere in the world. If you already have your own mobile, I strongly recommend that you do not use this for online/ business related activities.

As a suggestion, you may want to consider:

1) Buying a SIM card to use specifically for this, these days you can usually purchase these from your local newsagent of supermarket for £5 and can insert in your current handset when needed. Some companies also offer free SIM cards.

2) If you own a contract phone, ask your existing service provider how much it would cost to have a second phone number/ line routed to your current hand-set. This would allow you to keep your original line for personal calls and texts and the other line could be used for your online related activities.

3) Buy a pay as you go deal which includes a new handset and a SIM card. You even receive free credit on purchase with some offers.

- **Think of a basic letter head or visual image for yourself** – You do not have to commission a design house of printers to create artwork for you, even though after you discover that generating online income can be worthwhile you may want to give instructions for a professional brand or image to be created for you. For example if you decided to operate under "Silver Selections", you could create a letter head template using a simple type face and font in Microsoft Word. Alternatively, you could search for letterhead templates in Google or visit - http://office.microsoft.com/en-gb/templates/CT101043261033.aspx to start with.

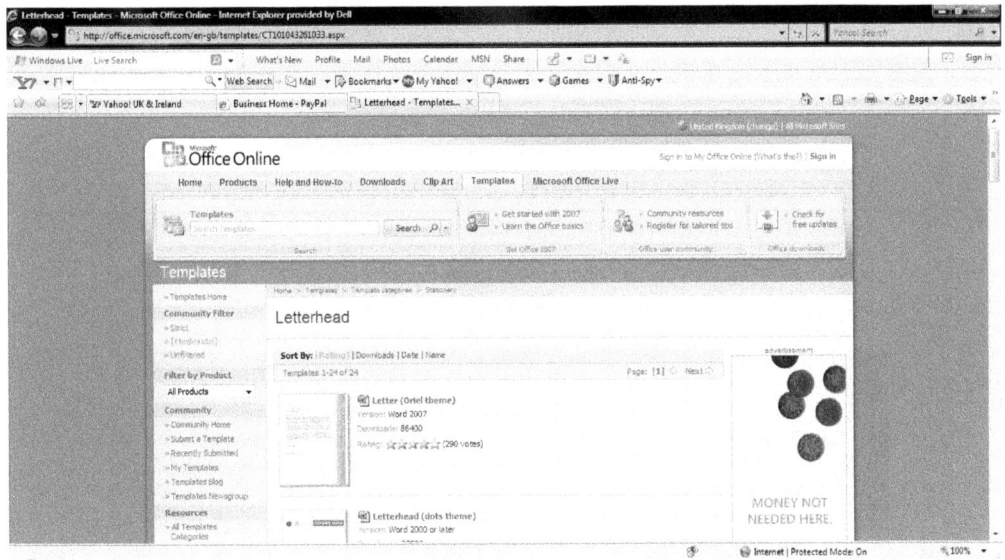

TASK – Consider doing and recording the above and by the end of it you should have:

A name to operate under such as "Silver Selections"
A dedicated email address
A dedicated phone number or mobile line
A letter head/ stationery to support the name you will be operating under

Back to creating your Pay Pal account

Now that you have decided this information, you can use this to create your Pay Pal account. Start off by visiting https://www.paypal-business.co.uk/ .

The following home page will appear:

- Click on the "Personal" tab marked as A below:

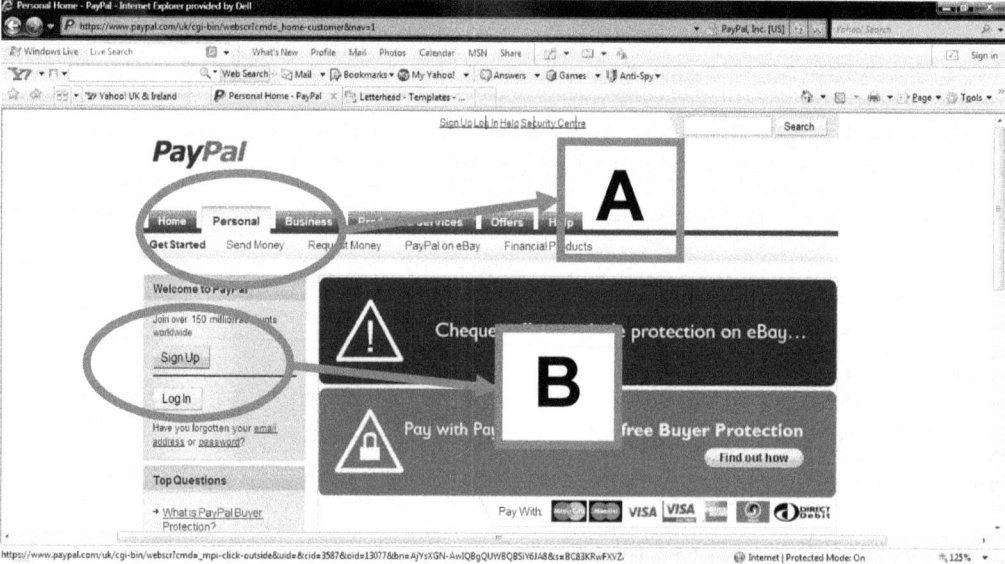

- Click on the "Sign up" button (marked B). The following page (below) will appear. Select the "Pay Pal for you" option (marked C) and complete the information in the sign up form.

- Remember that your first and last name will be the name you will operate under. For example, for the name Silver Selections,

"Silver" would be the first name and "Selections" would be the last name.

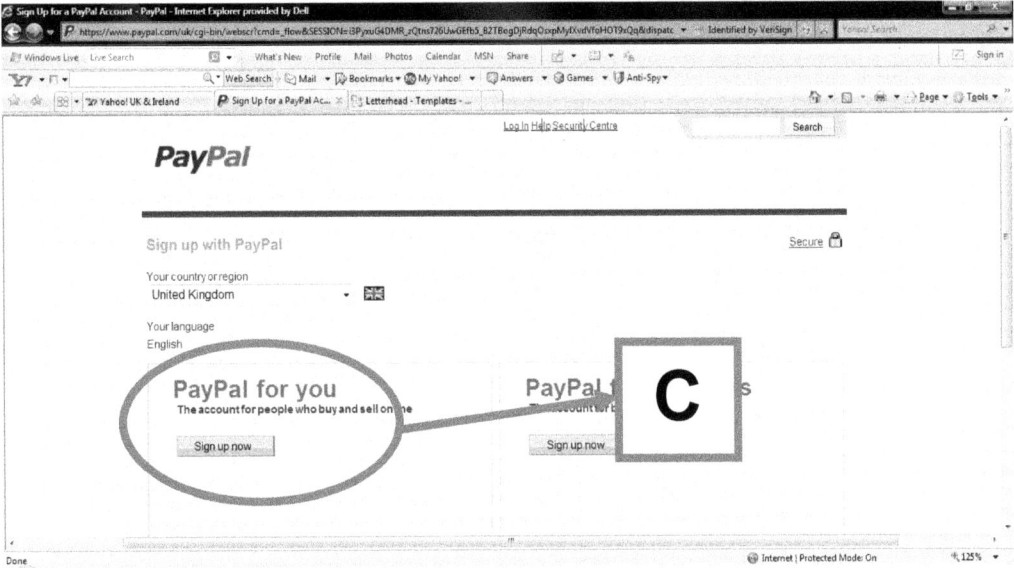

Chapter 3 – What will you need to create the income?

To re-cap from the previous chapter, so far you have:

- Been told what you will need to prepare/ get started.

- Created a name to operate under, including the creation of setting up a dedicated PO Box mailing address, an email address, mobile number and a letter head.

- Created a Pay Pal account so that online transactions can be accepted.

So what will you need to generate income to have the wedding that you *really* want?

Well now that you have prepared and set-up the basics, the next stage is to explain how you will generate enough income to have the wedding that you *really* want.

The following pages (and chapters) will offer guidance about how to generate automated streams of income online via a number of methods:

- Using Pay Per Click (PPC) advertising methods
- Joining Affiliate Programme Providers (APPs)
- Promoting services and products using your own websites

To maximise the use of these above online methods, first of all we have to define what products or services you can promote online. Once you follow the steps to set this up (and if done correctly) you will start to generate income even while you are asleep.

How to decide on what products or services you can promote

There are literally hundreds of products that can be promoted online. For those who are already familiar with generating automated income online, it is possible that going through a process of testing and exploring a variety of areas to generate a diverse portfolio of income has proven to be worthwhile. However, with anyone from established PLC companies to individuals creating their own income streams the most popular products and services are likely to be over promoted and saturated.

Finding a niche

I strongly suggest that you find a niche area to promote. As a general rule, it is easier to be a big fish in a small pond than to be a small fish in a large pond. In other words it is easier to create demand in a niche (or potential area) than to attempt to fill the demand that everyone else is attempting to fill too.

Over the next few pages, I will offer a suggestion of how you can create or identify a niche area to focus on so that you can generate the income to pay for the wedding you *really* want.

STEP 1 - It is all about you

To get you started, grab your designated notebook for your online income (as previously advised) and then think about and record the following:

- What age range do you fit in?
- What is your social, educational and ethnic background?
- What is your income or current salary?
- What are your core interests and/ or hobbies?
- Where are you located? E.g. England, Ireland, Scotland, Wales, Overseas
- Are you a homeowner?

Think about this as much as possible. By doing this, you have created a potential customer profile of who would buy the services or products you are going to promote online to generate income for the wedding you *really* want. You may find it helpful to record this information in a table like this:

Example profile of "Marie":

Section	Answers
Age	28
Education level	BA (Hons)
Gender	Female
Career/ Job	Teacher – Head of English
Membership of any professional groups or industries	TDA, Teacher's Union
Salary band	£35k - £45k
Values	"Give respect to get it."
Geographical location	North London, UK
Preferred magazines and newspapers	TES, Vogue, Cosmopolitan, Making Jewellery
Interests	Hair, cosmetics, beauty, performing arts/ musicals/ shows, Accessories and Fashion. Eating in recommended restaurants – middle end to high end standard, overseas travel.
Social groups	Church, work colleagues, friends from dance classes
Ethnicity	English and West Indian heritage

By using this information about yourself, create a general customer profile. For example from Marie's profile above we can create the following customer profile:

Section	Answers	Images
Age range:	25 - 35	
Education level	Educated to BA or BSc (Hons) and possibly at postgraduate level	
Gender	Female	

Career/ job	Qualified and/ or experienced Professionals – Middle Leaders, Solicitors, Teachers, Project Managers, Accountants	
Membership to any professional groups or industries	Project management, Child Protection, Education, Advertising/ Media/ Communications, Law	
Salary band	£35k - £45k	
Values	Believes in God/ strong faith; believes in the principle of giving; believes in delivering standards of excellence.	
Family	Possibly has 0-2 children, married, single or in a relationship	
Geographical location	Large cities in the UK. E.g. London, Birmingham Leeds, Manchester Glasgow, Edinburgh etc.	

Preferred magazines and newspapers	Pride, Cosmopolitan, Hello, Ebony, OK magazine, Asian Woman, Vogue	
Interests	Hair, cosmetics, beauty, performing arts/ musicals/ shows, Accessories and Fashion. Eating in recommended restaurants – middle end to high end standard, like to travel overseas.	
Social groups	Church, work colleagues, volunteer groups/ peers etc	
Ethnicity	Cosmopolitan - including English, European, Black, Mixed Race, Asian, Indian etc.	

TIP – Do you remember your Wedding storyboard that you created in chapter 1? Consider finding images of people who fit the profile that is similar to yours.

What sectors or markets are of interest to you and your new customer profile?

TASK – List the top three areas or markets that are of interest to you. Let's refer to the example of the customer profile that we created from Marie. Let's focus on two areas:

- Membership to any professional groups or industries
- Interests

From this information, as an example "Marie" could choose to focus on:

- Travel
- Beauty & Cosmetics
- Fashion

Do the same. Note these top three areas in your notebook so that these notes can be a clear point of reference.

Going narrow and deep

Now that you have your top three areas that you could focus on and your overall customer profile, it's time to think a little more specifically.

To illustrate how you can define what products or goods to promote so that you can generate online income to get the wedding that you *really* want, we'll use an example from our fantasy profile lady Marie.

From Marie's list of top three areas of focus, let's focus on Beauty & Cosmetics.

With an industry that is worth millions of pounds (and dollars), there are a number of Beauty and Cosmetic products that you could locate and promote. So where do you start? It's time to get narrow and deep!

The best thing to do is to focus on a specific area and then get so specific that it has the ability for you to create greater demand or interest rather than to try and compete with the high street retailers and big brands. Using Marie's focus of Beauty & Cosmetics, Marie decides that she wants to focus on promoting shampoo to begin with. Here's an example of how an everyday product can become specific to meet the needs of a niche market or customer:

Basic Beauty Product:	Break down of product to make it semi-specific	Breakdown of the product to make it specific:	Breakdown of the product to make it appeal to a niche group:
Shampoo	Shampoo for: Curly hair Dry hair Breaking hair etc.	Shampoo for: Curly hair with enriched vitamins A & E	Shampoo for Curly hair, enriched with vitamins A & E made from 100% organic ingredients
Suitable for:	Every day use, general consumer	A customer who is willing to pay for a specific hair product with incentives or specific features	A customer who is willing to pay a premium for a product that meets all their needs, but which has extraordinary elements, in this case "organic ingredients."

The more specific the product or service is the more that you can expect to charge for that service or product.

So for this example, Marie decides that she would like to promote a new range of shampoo products, i.e.

- Organic Shampoo with enriched vitamins A & E for curly hair
- Organic shampoo with enriched vitamins A & E for breaking hair
- Organic shampoo with enriched vitamins A & E for chemically treated hair

- The list could go on and get more specific

TASK – By using the example above think about a range of products or services you would take interest in. For example you may decide to initially focus on "beauty" but then to focus on body lotions for sensitive skin.

Defining how popular the search term for your product category service is

There are a number of ways of finding out intelligence regarding what terms and keywords people in the UK and around the world use to locate information and items they want. For example:

- www.keyworddiscovery.com
- www.wordtracker.com
- www.keywordelite.com
- www.keywordanalyzer.com

You will find that if you go to www.google.com and type in the words of something that you are looking for, it will summarise the number of relevant pieces of information that relate to the words you are inputting into Google. This appears in a list like the one below:

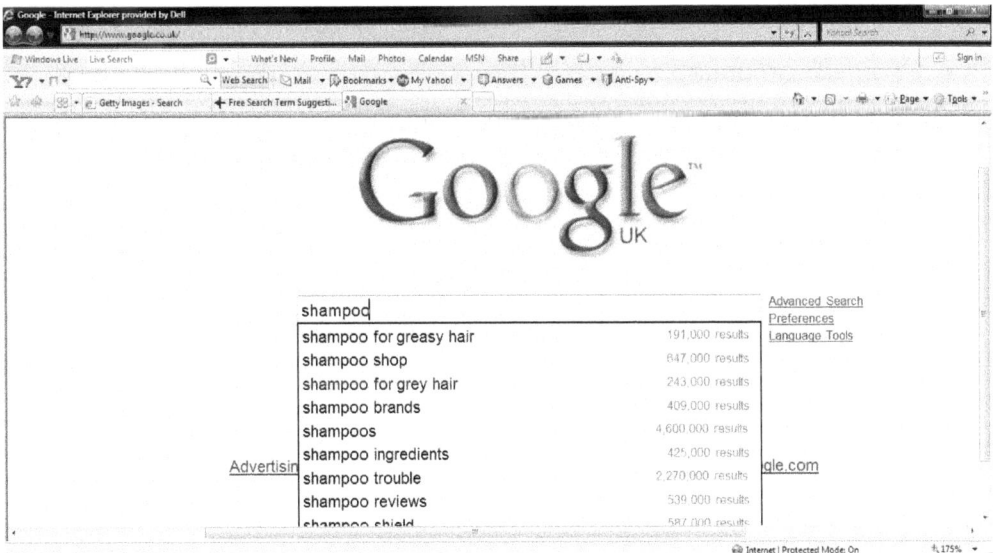

Using Keyword Discovery

Using Marie's example of deciding to focus her first income stream to promote shampoo, let's get an indication of how popular the keyword "Shampoo" is used:

- Go to www.keyworddiscovery.com . The following home page should appear:

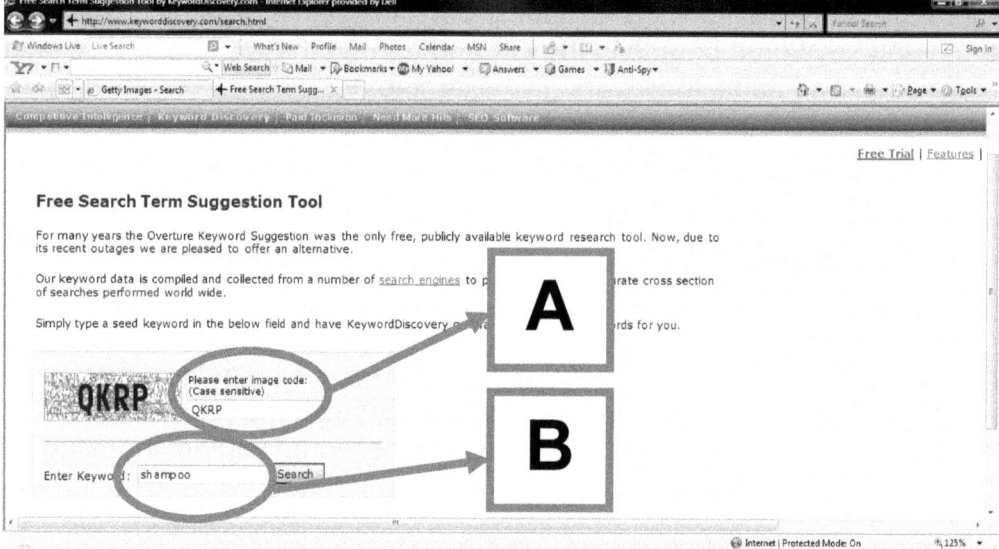

- You will be asked to type in the code (marked A) into the blank field to the right and then type in your keyword, in this case "Shampoo" (marked as B) and click the "Search" button.

- The following page will appear. This page offers a summarised indication of the number of times that the keyword "shampoo" is used by people searching and browsing the internet.

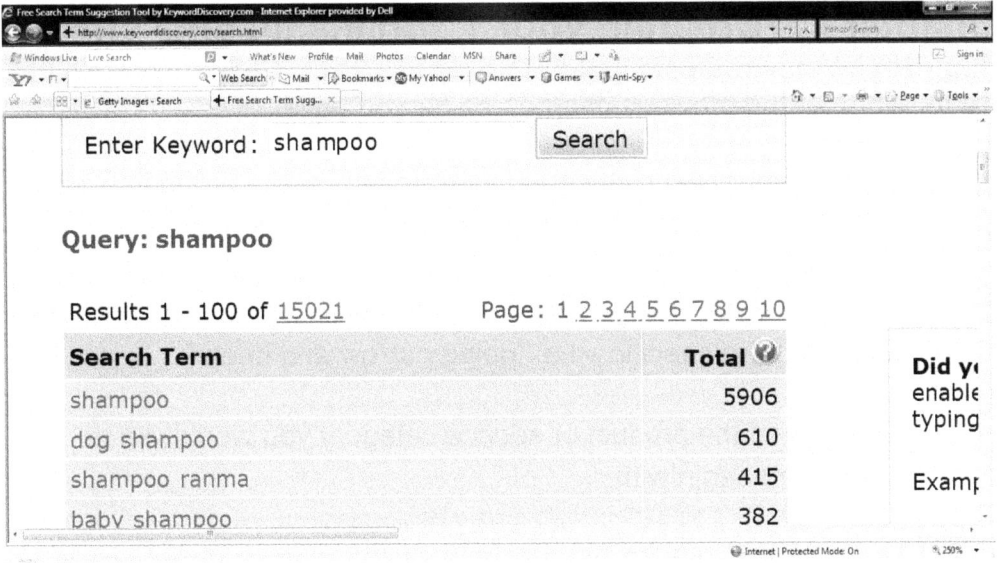

TASK – Once you decide which product category, products or services you would like to promote search for the keywords linked to the areas you want to work in.

TIP – Conducting key note searches can also assist you with reviewing other possible niche areas and decide how this can be tailored and advertised to your identiifed customer profile that you created earlier. After you conduct your keyword searches, be sure to record what the keyword(s) are and the number of times a keyword is used. Make a note of the date as well as the website that you used to determine these statistics. **These will help you when you start to advertise, which will be covered later on in this book.**

Why do I need to determine keywords?

The keywords that you have identified for the categories you want to promote and/ or sell will be used in your online marketing and advertising campaigns and more importantly they will feature in the website, blog or Twitter links that you will create to specifically promote the products and services that you want.

So what's next? It's time to create your 1st online income stream so that you can pay for the wedding that you *really* want!

Chapter 4 – Creating your 1st online income stream

To re-cap from the previous chapter, so far you have:

- Created your own niche customer profile, i.e. the group you will promote your products and/ or services to.

- Discovered how to make an everyday product (also applicable to a service) more specific – i.e. "going narrow and deep."

- Determined the product or service category you would like to promote to begin with.

- Learnt how to use keyword search sites to determine keywords that you will use to feed into your websites and other online promoting/ advertising methods.

STEP 1 – Creating your 1st website for promoting products and/ or services

There are a number of websites that offer you the opportunity to be able to buy a professional looking web domain; however this is not necessary for you to be able to generate online income. At a later stage if and when you become more confident, you will be able to invest more money into purchasing an actual domain name.

FREE Websites

The free websites that I recommend to help you start include:

- www.350.com

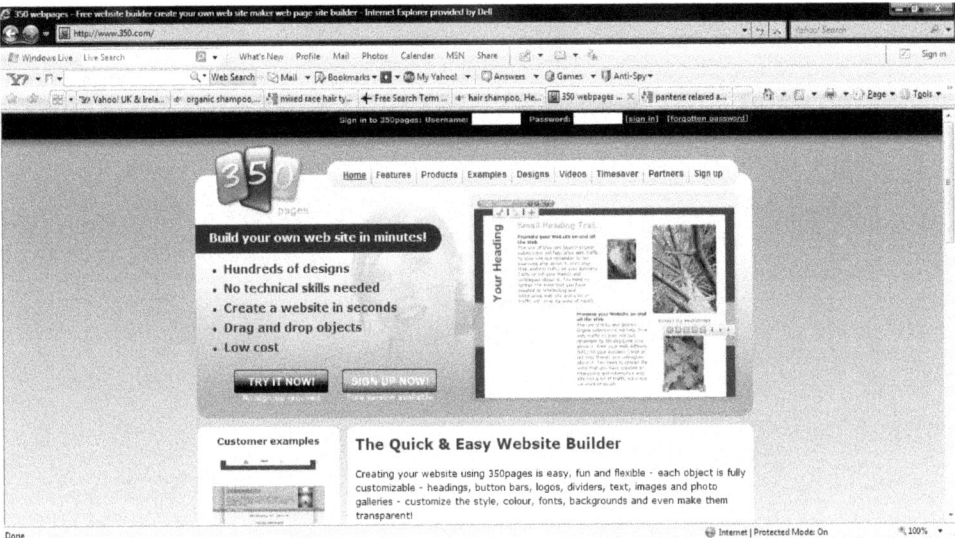

- www.yola.com

- www.weebly.com

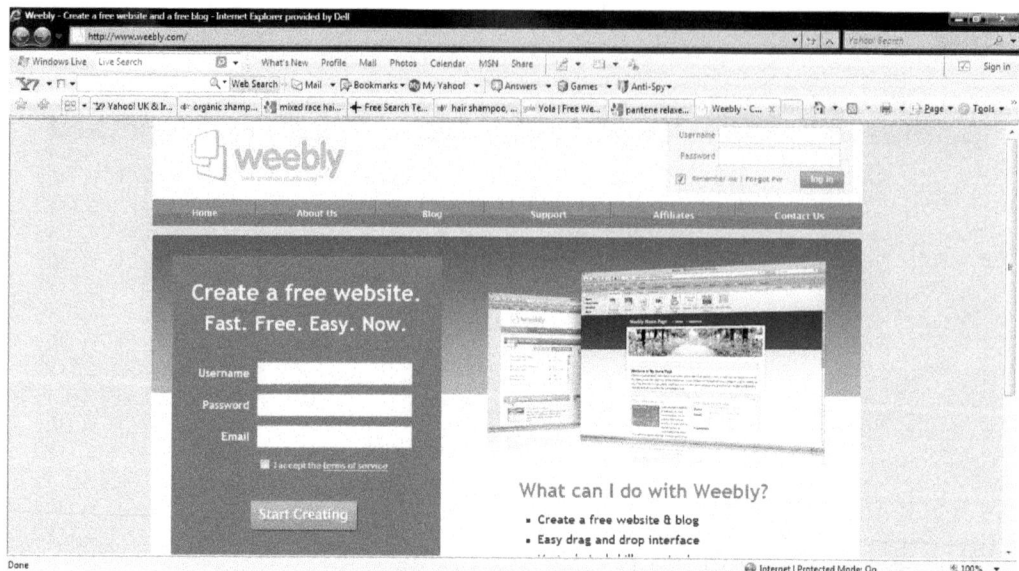

There are plenty more website providers, but for the sake of simplicity, using weebly.com will be used to show you how you can create your own website within 60 – 120 minutes.

Let's continue to use Marie whose customer profile we used to decide that shampoo would be the beauty and cosmetics product that she wants to promote.

Let's get started!

- Connect to your internet and go to www.weebly.com

You need to create a username and password, so make sure that you create your account using something you will remember.

TIP – REMEMBER this will be your first online income stream (of many), so remember to securely record your username and passwords each time. You can record the usernames and passwords in your dedicated notebook. When you sign in you can also use your dedicated email address that you created in chapter 2.

- Once you have registered, the following page will appear:

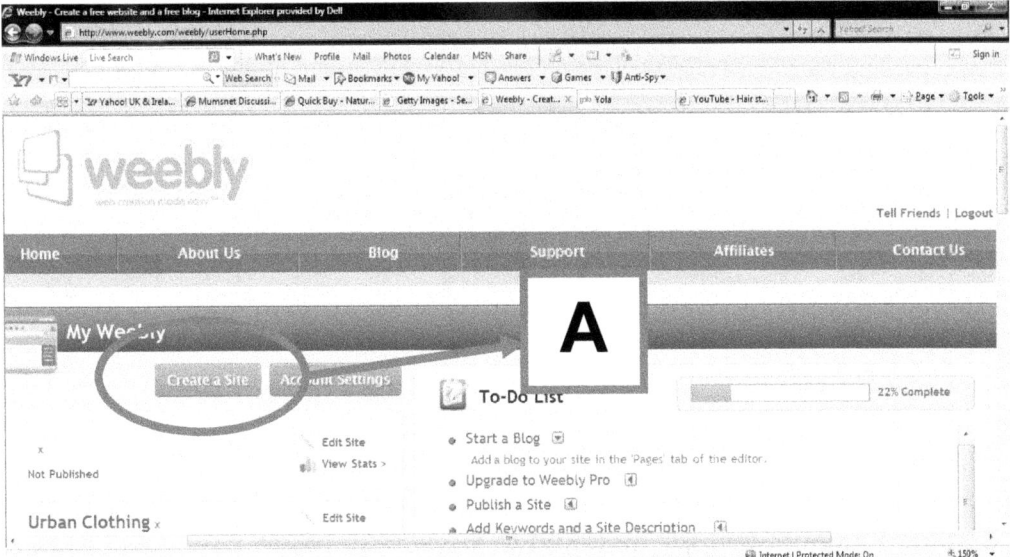

- Click on the "Create a site" button marked as A. A pop-up screen will appear "Title Your New Site" marked as B (see below).

TIP – When you are naming your website, remember to use the keyword(s) that you have identified in the previous chapter(s). For example, if you want your site to be based on organic shampoo, you would name it "Organic shampoos."

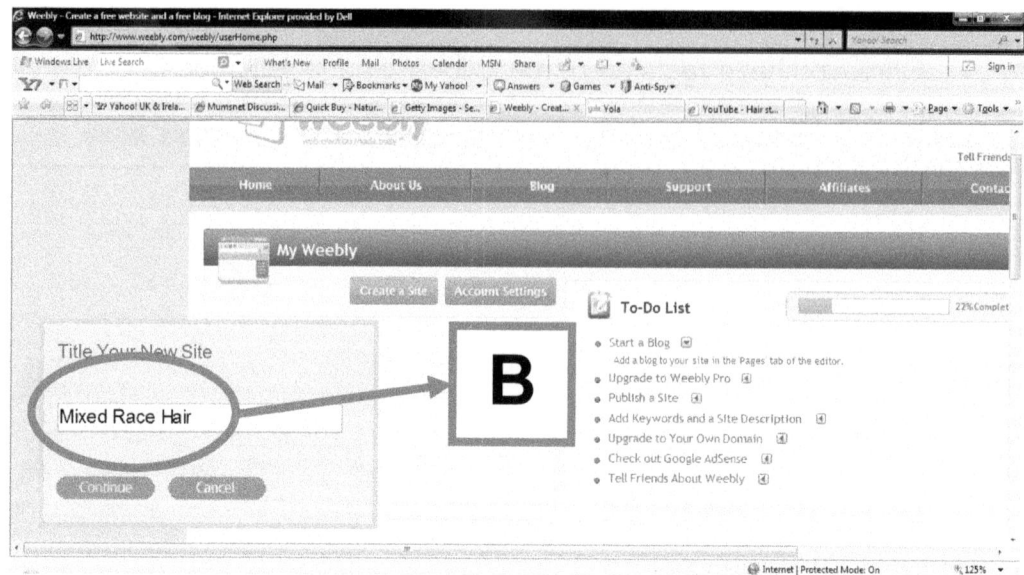

For this example, the site is called "Mixed Race Hair." Once you click the "Continue" button, you will be taken to the screen below:

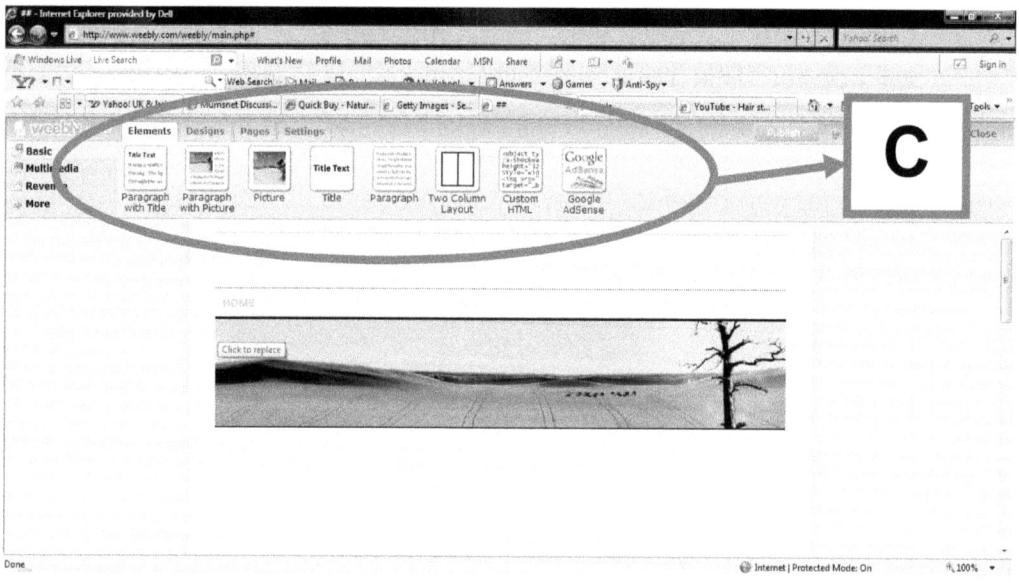

Your website will be made of "Elements." There are 7 elements or tools you can use to build the page(s) on your site, marked as C. These include:

- Paragraph with Title
- Paragraph with Picture

- Picture
- Title Text
- Paragraph
- Two column layout
- Custom HTML
- Google Adsense

Any of these elements can be selected and dragged onto your page. Place your mouse over the element you want to use, click and hold down the left button on your mouse and drag down to the page of your site.

How to change the page design of your website

At the moment, the page design features a header with a tree design. There are a number of designs you can choose.

- Click on the "Designs" tab at the top of the page to the left. A sequence of page designs will appear across the top of the page, marked as D:

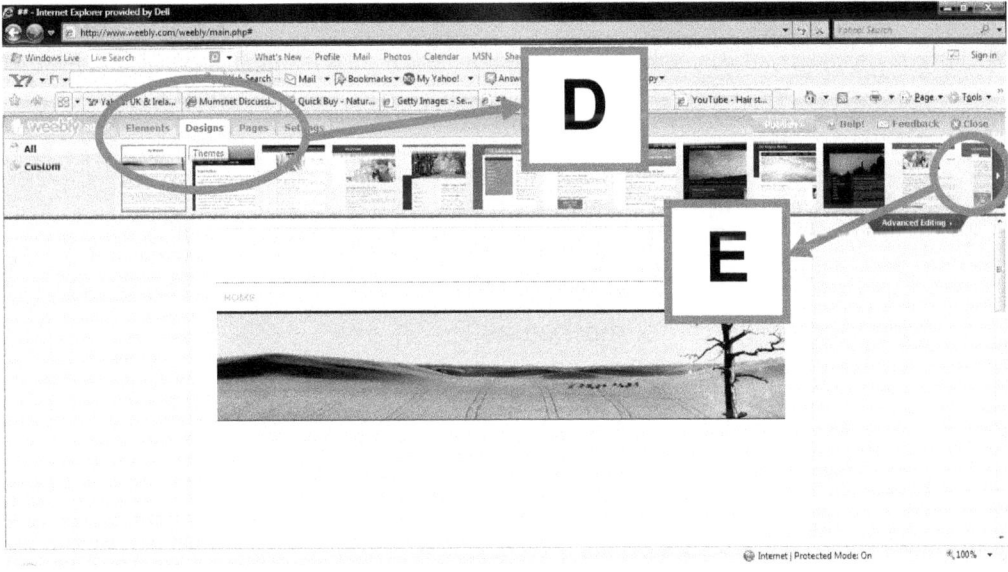

- You can select the next set of page design options by clicking on the arrow marked as E.

- Once you decide on the page design that you want, double click on it and it will then be loaded on your website page.

- For this example, a flower design below has been chosen (see below). If you click on the "Elements" tab again, you can click on the element you want to place on your page by selecting the element and dragging it onto the page.

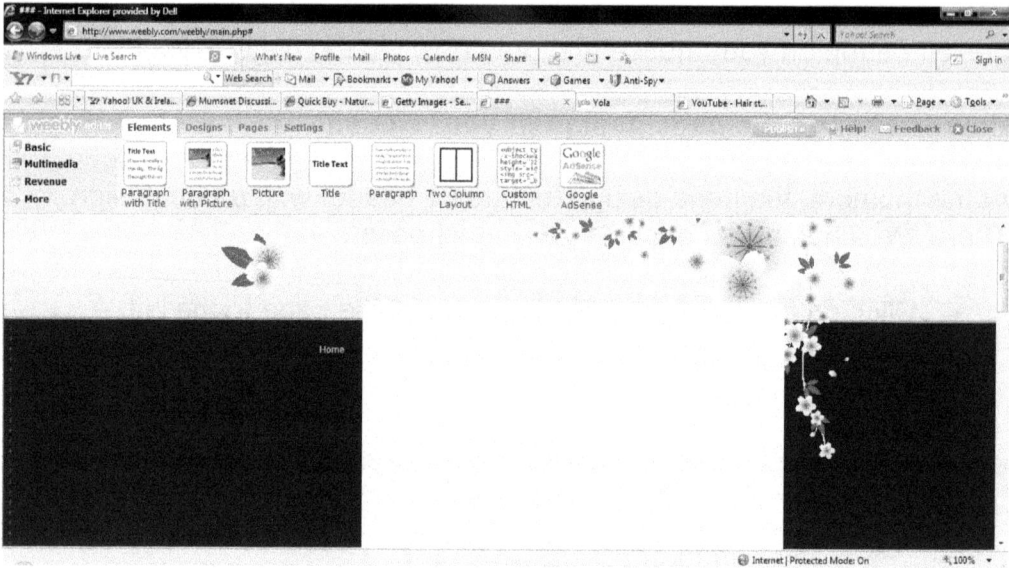

TIP – Whenever you roll over an element, a pop up message will appear instructing you to drag it to the page.

- For this example, the element "Paragraph with picture" has been dragged to the page, marked as F.

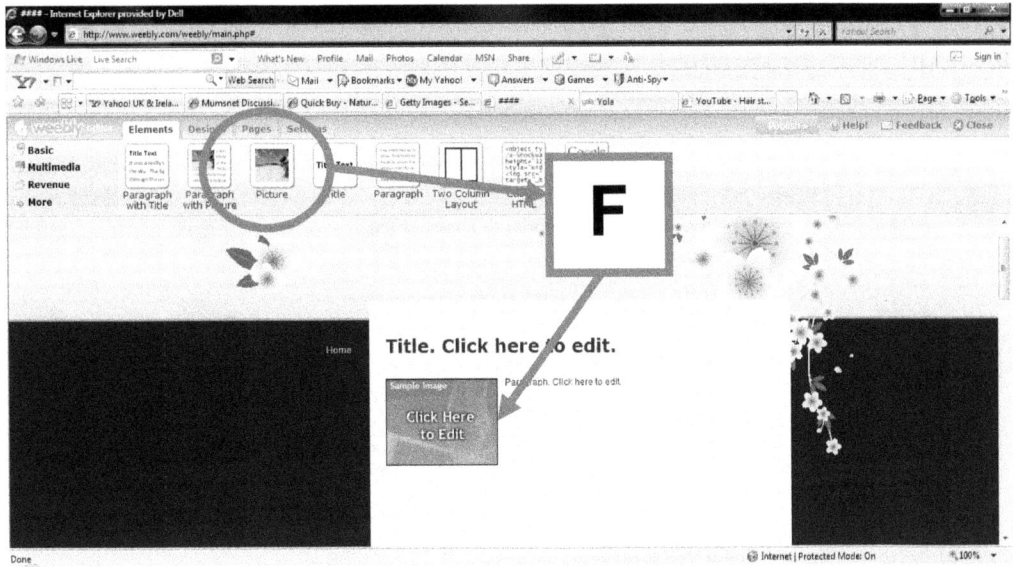

- Now, the title can be edited and a picture can be inserted. Text can also be typed alongside the image as a paragraph.

- Click on the section that you want to edit, make or add the changes and these will be changed automatically.

- To add a picture or photo, click on the blue box titled "Click here to edit." A link will appear in the edit bar – "Upload new image" so that you can upload an image (marked G). Images can be uploaded from your computer or laptop that has been stored previously.

TIP – If you do not have any relevant images stored previously on your computer or laptop, you can source images from a number of sites, including:

www.istockphoto.com
www.gettyimages.com
http://www.dreamstime.com

When you find an image that you want, place your mouse over the image and right click and select the option "Save picture as" and store this on your computer or laptop.

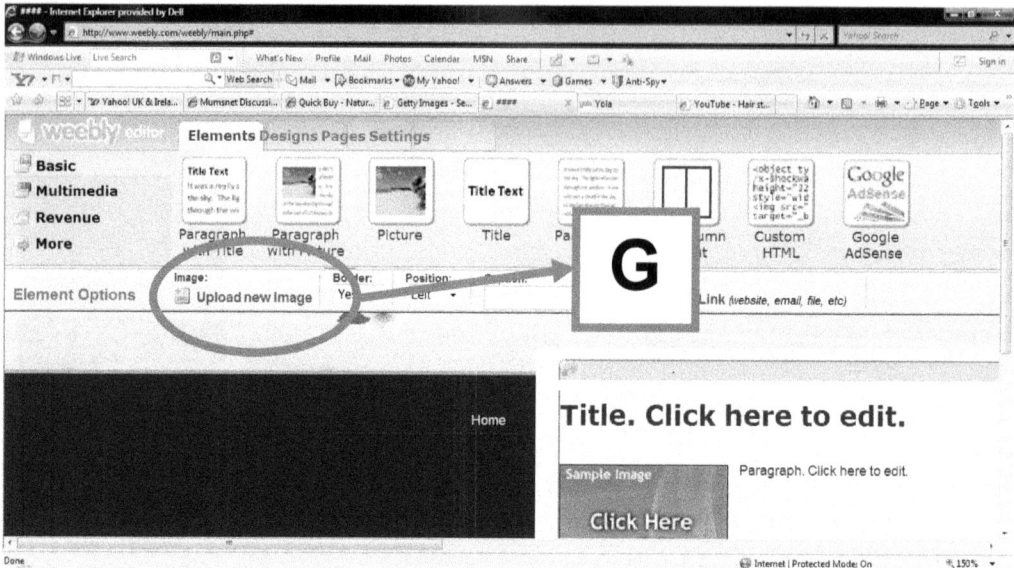

- Next, click on "Paragraph. Click here to edit" and type in the text you want to feature on your home page. An example marked H features below:

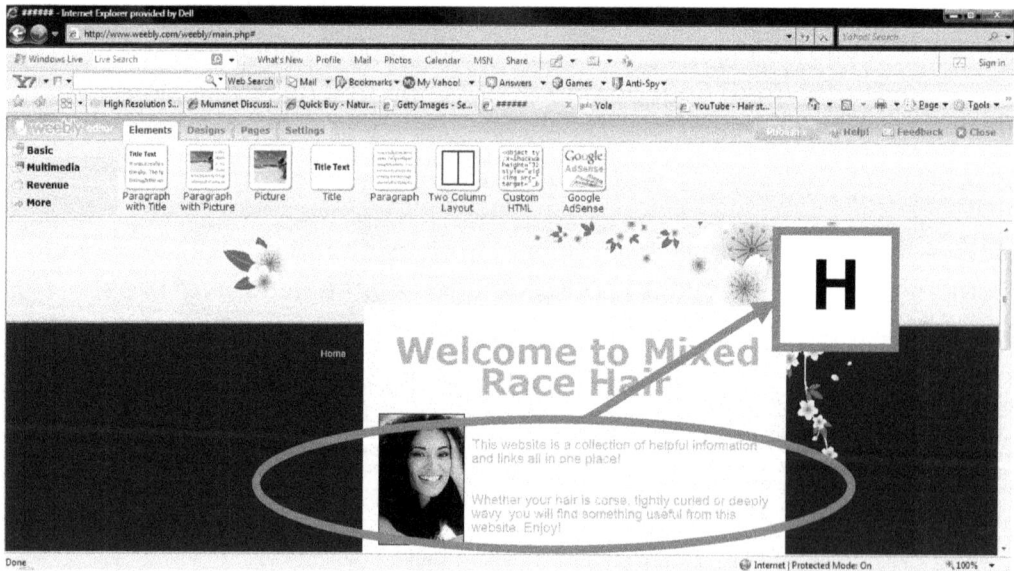

Adding a video onto your website

For your website you can search for videos and material to support the products or services that you want to promote on your website.

- First of all go to www.youtube.com and select a video that suits your website.

- In the search box, type in keywords. For this example, "mixed race hair tips" was searched for marked as I.

- You will need the address of this video (marked J) to add to your website in just a moment.

- To add video to your website, click on the Multimedia link to the left of the screen marked K:

47

- Now drag the You Tube icon (marked L below) onto your website page in the position that you would like it to appear on the page.

- A default video will appear to the left of the page in the edit bar (marked M below). Remember the address to the You Tube video you found earlier, select and paste this address into the "You Tube video URL" field.

- Click outside of the edit bar and the video you want to show will load onto your website page automatically.

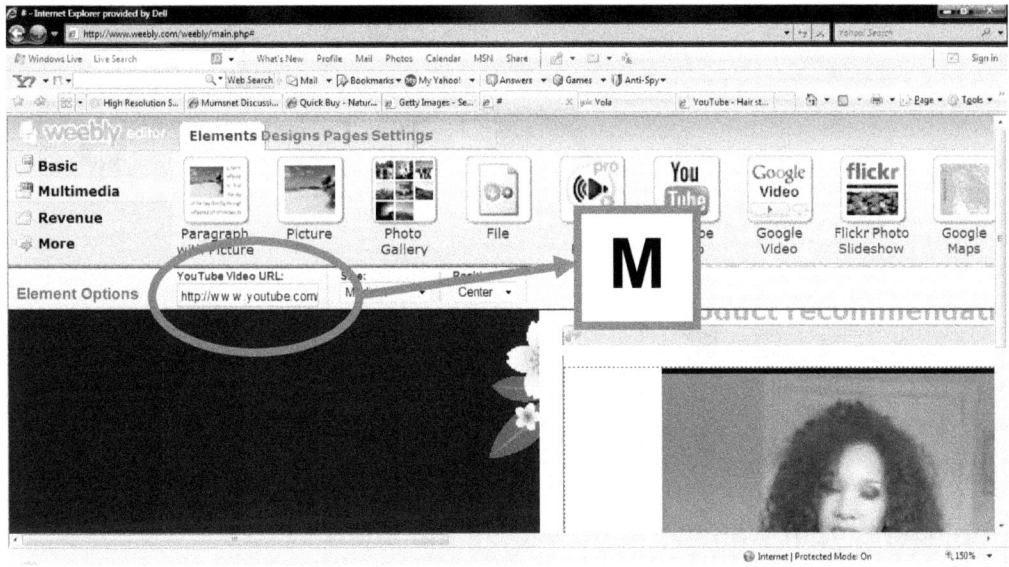

Adding more pages to your website

It is possible to use your home page as the only page that you need to promote the products and/ or services that you want. In this example, additional pages were added to this website:

- Hair Care Products
- Hair Care Tips
- Articles & More Info

To create new/ additional pages to your website:

- At the top of the page, click on the "Pages" tab and the following screen will appear titled "Manage Pages."

- Click on the "New Page" button (marked as N) and a text box will appear that will initially say "New Page" marked as O. Type in the name of your new page and click the "Save" button marked as P to create your new page.

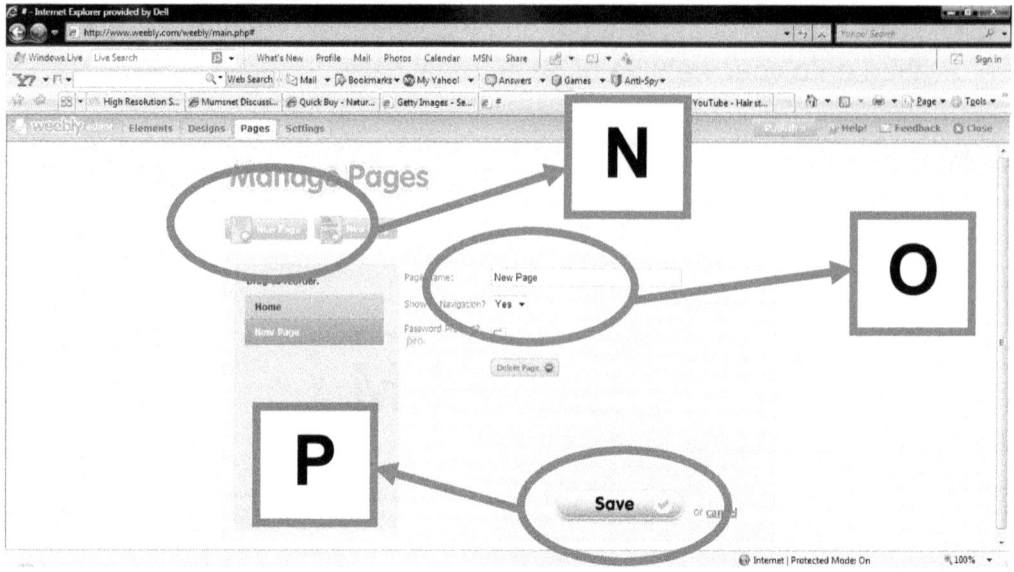

Publishing your website to go live on the internet

Do not worry if you feel that your web pages are unfinished you have 24 hour access to view and edit your web pages as long as you have internet access.

To publish the page(s) of the site that you have done so far:

- Click on the "Settings" tab and click on the link titled "Change site address" marked as Q.

- Change your website address using the keywords you identified in chapter 3. In this example, the website is named www.mixedracehair.weebly.com.

TIP – You can purchase a full domain name so that your website does not feature on the internet including "Weebly" (i.e. it will read as www.mixedracehair.com) however, you would have to pay a fee for this domain. Also, please note that this is your first online income stream. As you gain more experience and source other suppliers and providers (and income) you will be able to invest in domain names to suit you.

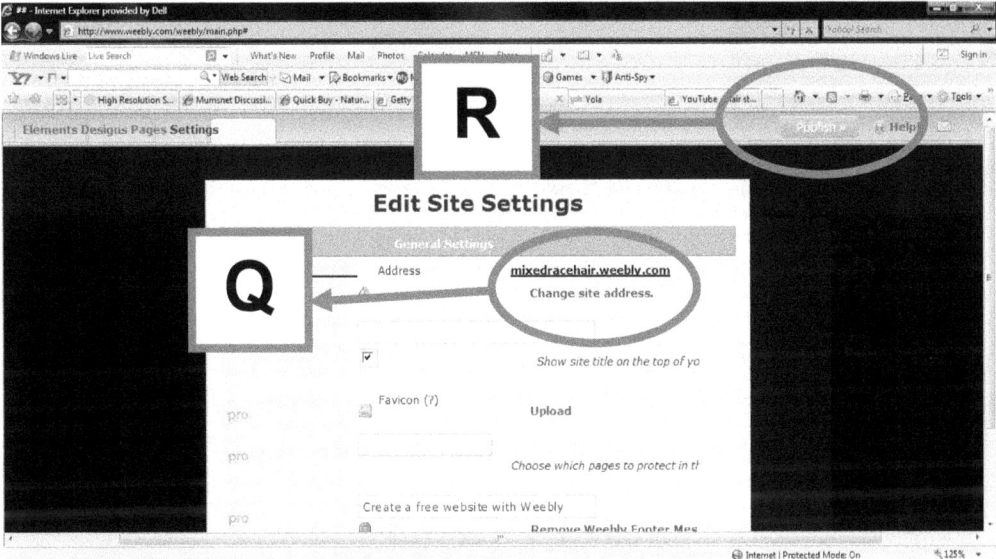

- Remember to save any changes you make, by scrolling down to the end of the page and click on the "Save" button.

- Next the screen will return to the page of your website. Click on the "Publish" button (marked R) if you are happy with what you have done.

- The following pop-up should appear on the screen below:

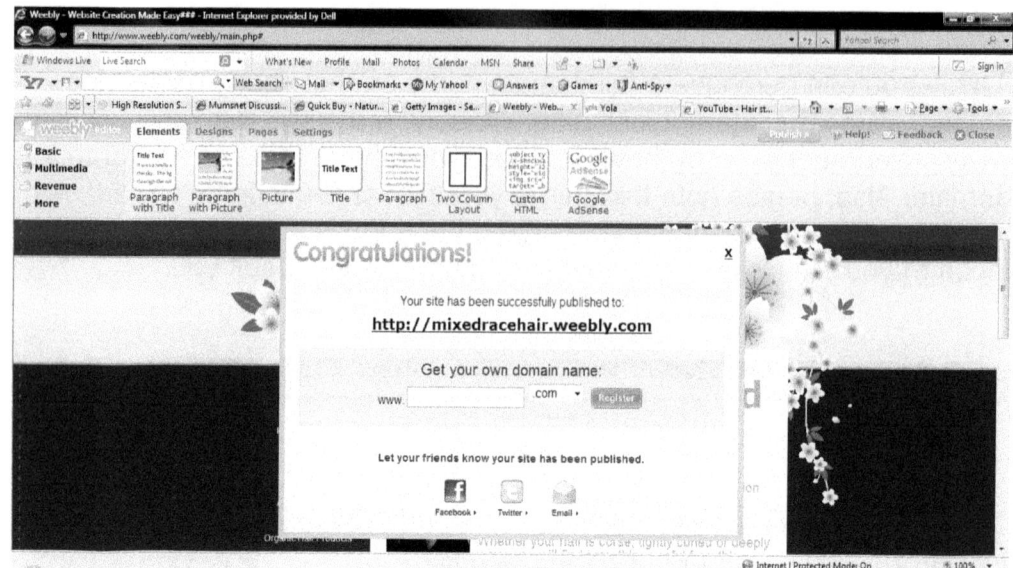

CONGRATULATIONS!

You have published your first domain to generate online income to pay for the wedding that you *really* want. Take a break! You have gone through the pain barrier of getting familiar with new territory.

WELL DONE!

Chapter 5 – Creating auction links and more to add to your website

To re-cap from the previous chapter, so far you have:

- Created your own website dedicated specifically to the product or service category that you identified in previous chapters

- Published or made your own website live on the internet

Checking your keywords with Traffic Estimator

In chapter 3, keyword websites were introduced to you, which can enable the search of keyword(s) linked specifically for the product and/ or services category.

To remain consistent, the example of Mixed Race Hair (i.e. in reference to the website that was demonstrated – www.mixedracehair.weebly.com) will be used again to show how keywords can be compared.

Results for the search terms "mixed race hair" on Keyworddiscovery.com follow:

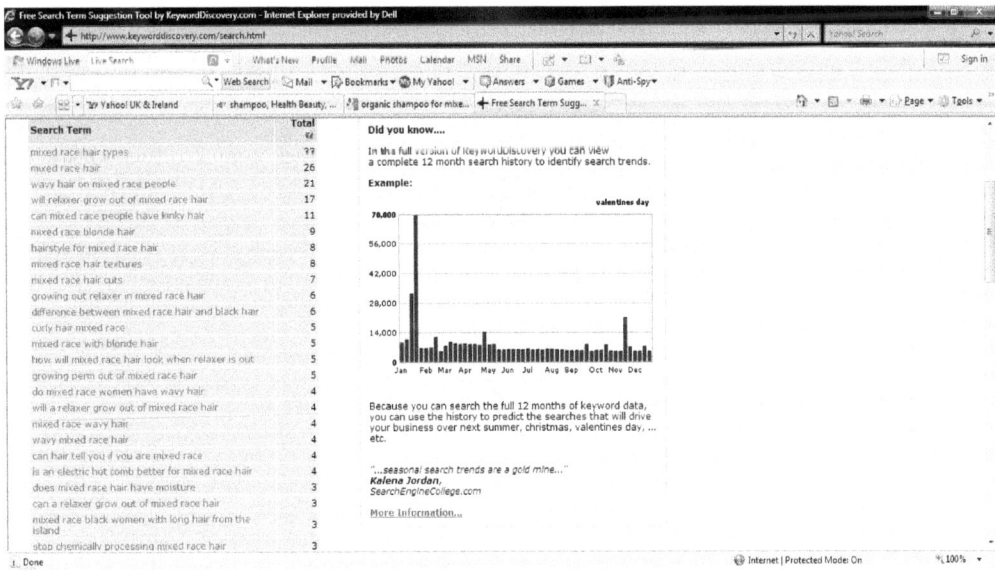

According to Keyword Discovery, the keyword "Mixed race hair" was searched for 26 times.

If we visit Google's Traffic Estimator at
https://adwords.google.com/select/TrafficEstimatorSandbox , we can see what results Google advise.

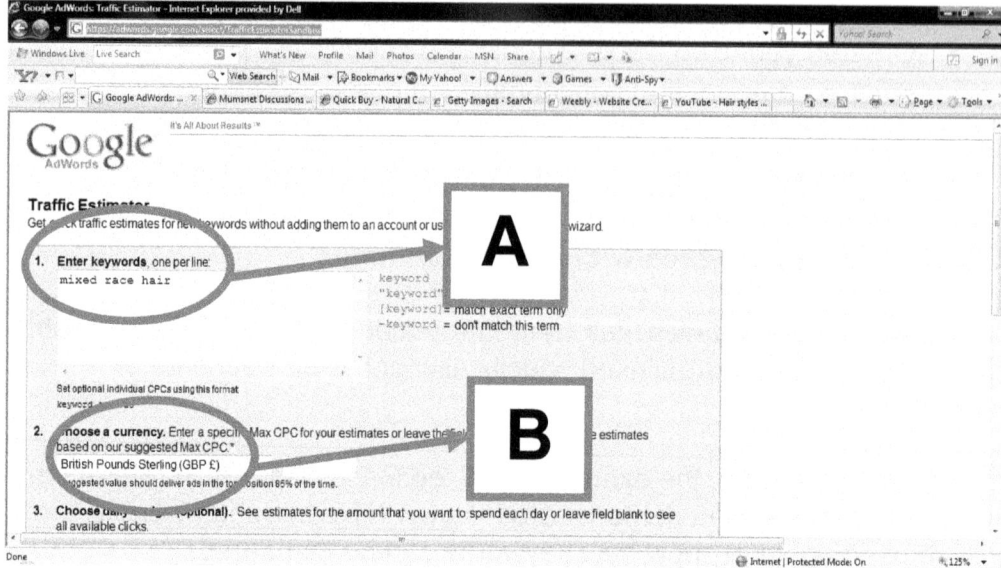

- Complete all the fields, marked A (type in your keyword(s) and B (select your currency).

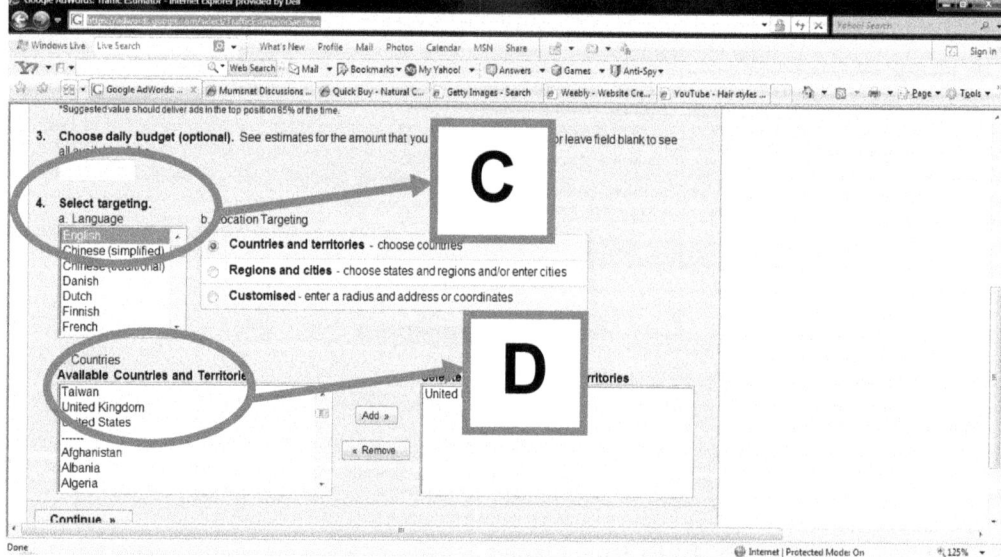

- Complete all the fields marked C (select your language) and D (select UK on the left, click the "Add" button and then click the continue button).

The page below should appear. Google estimates that this search term should receive 1 click per day using Google's PPC (Pay Per Click) advertising – i.e. via adverts that are created using Google Adwords adverts. (This is marked as E).

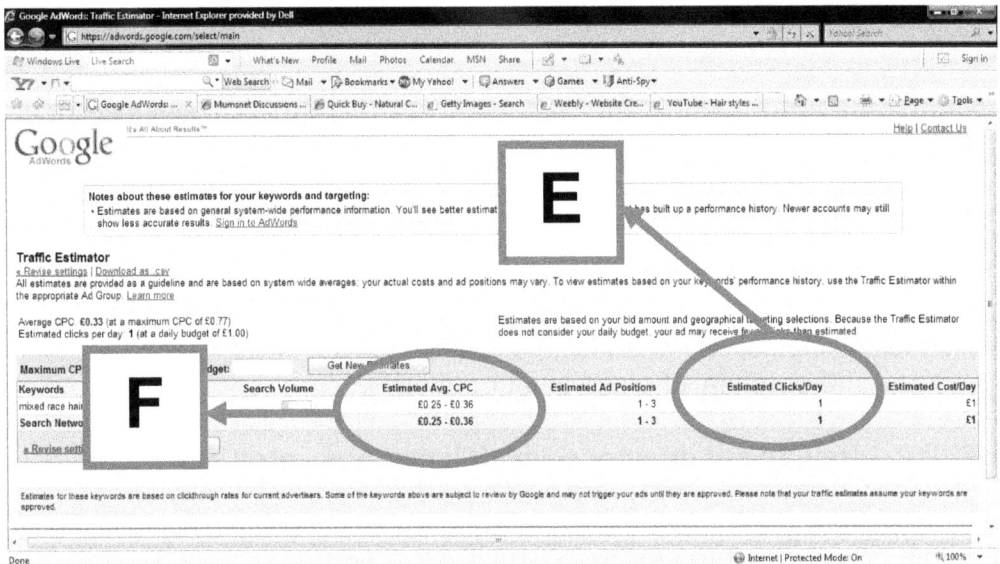

Google also estimates that the top bidder for this advertising spot is currently paying £0.36 (marked as F).

TIP – These figures are estimates only and depending on what you are promoting, the rates that you pay each time someone who searches Google clicks on one of your adverts will vary. This can be as low as £0.02.

At the time of searching for "mixed race hair" in a Google search for the UK, it showed the following Google Adwords adverts marked as G:

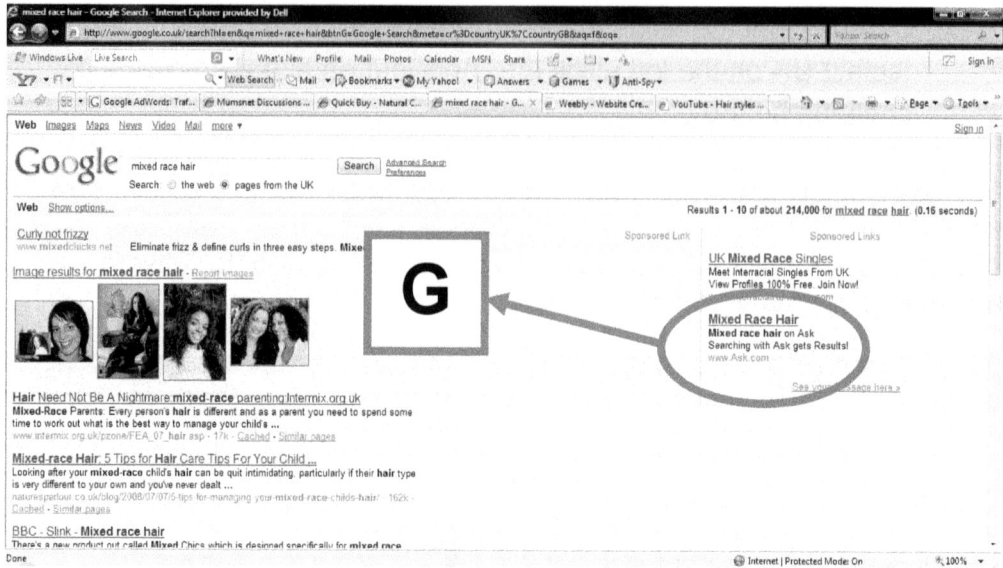

The screen shows that the Adwords adverts that were in the top positions were held by the search engine - www.ask.com and a dating site for UK mixed race singles. It is important to know what adverts exist so that you can know the potential of placing your advert.

STEP 2 – How to set up your own affiliate links using eBay

The website that you have created can be used to feature and promote products that are available on eBay.

To join eBay's affiliate programme is free! All it involves is registering your details. You will need the information that you set up before - i.e. your dedicated email address, the name you are operating under or the name of your company (if you have decided to register one) and the website that you have created for free that you will use to promote your first online income. First of all:

- Connect to the internet and go to www.eBay.co.uk and scroll down the page to find the link for "Affiliates" marked as H below.

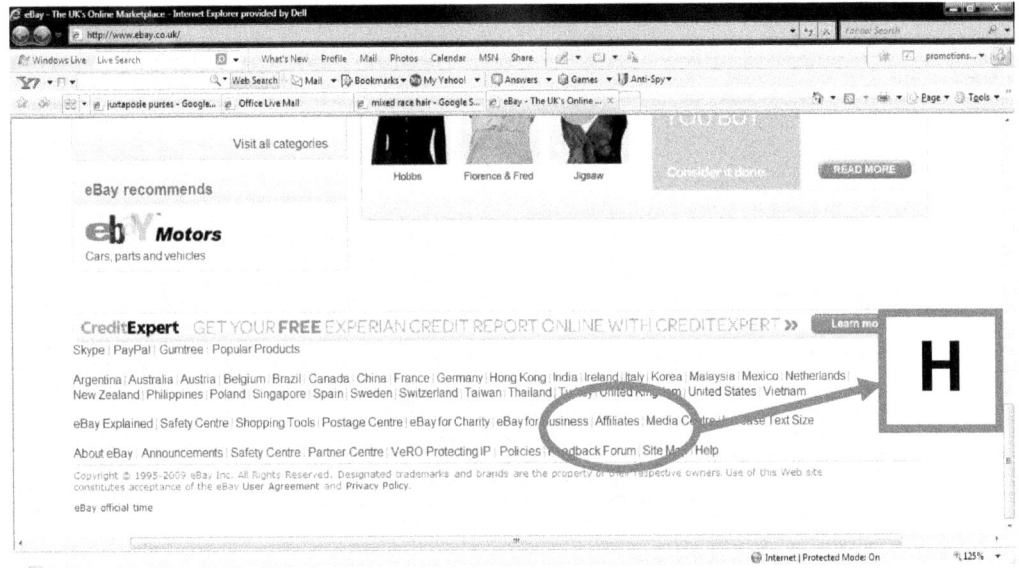

- Alternatively, type in this link to go straight to the registration page - https://www.ebaypartnernetwork.com/files/hub/en-US/index.html?alt=uk

- Click on the "Join Now" button marked as I.

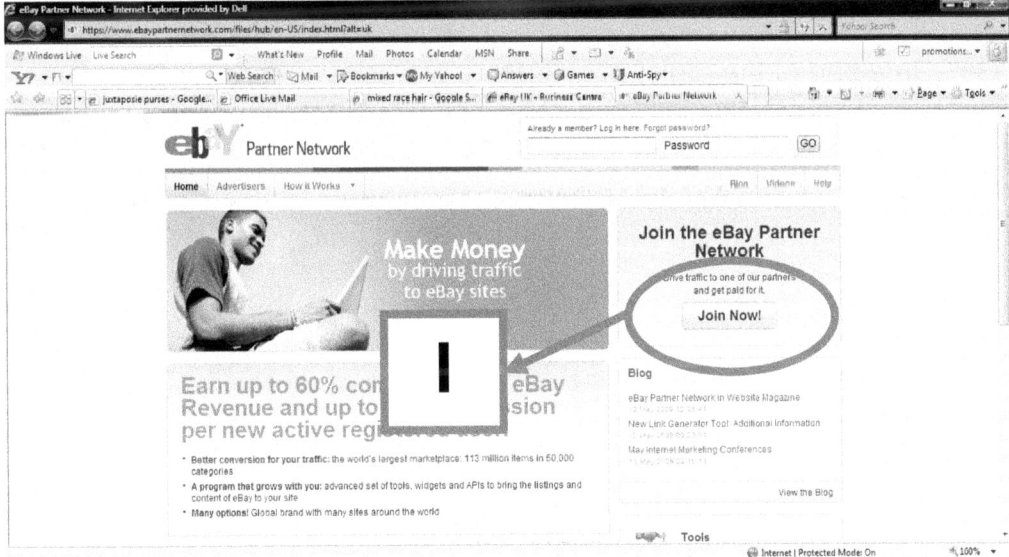

- The link will take you through to a page of terms and conditions that you must accept before being able to register. Once completed scroll down and click the "Continue" button marked J.

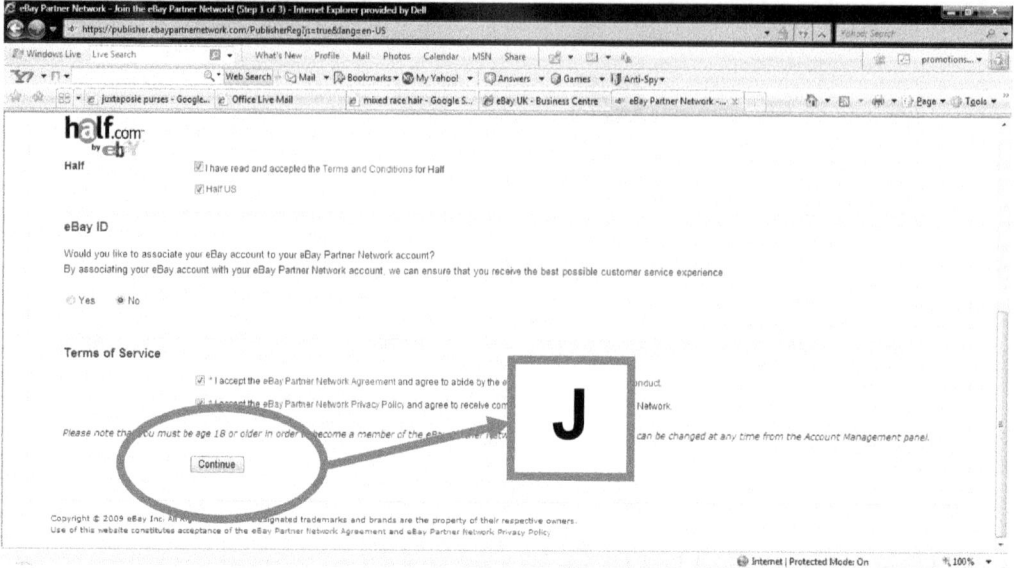

- Next the page below will appear.

- You will be expected to register your details, so you will need the email address you created before, confirm your full name, and your newly created website address.

TIP: On a part of the registration form, it will ask you for your Business Name, if you have decided on a name you would like to operate under (for example mine is "Purple Panel"), then you will have to state your full name.

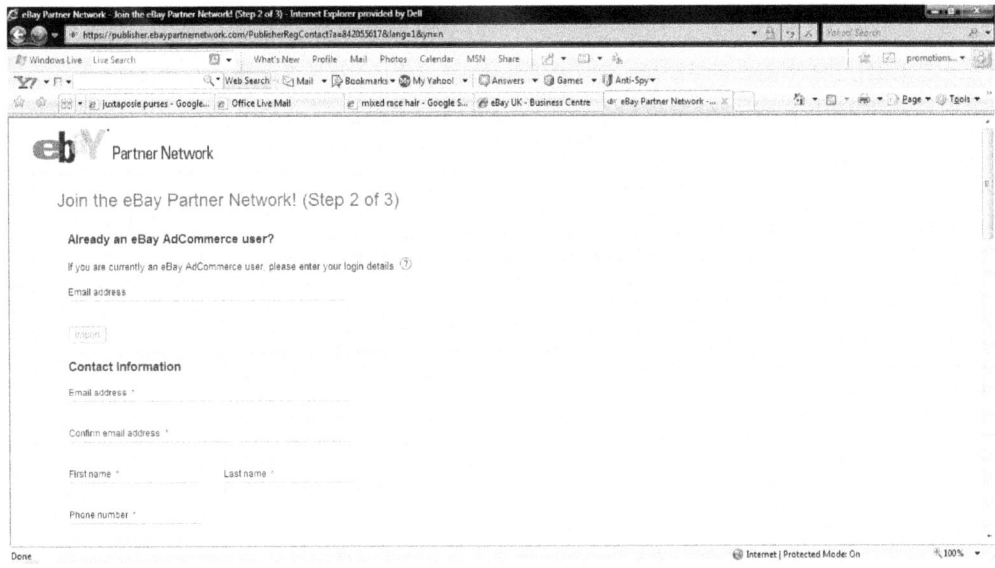

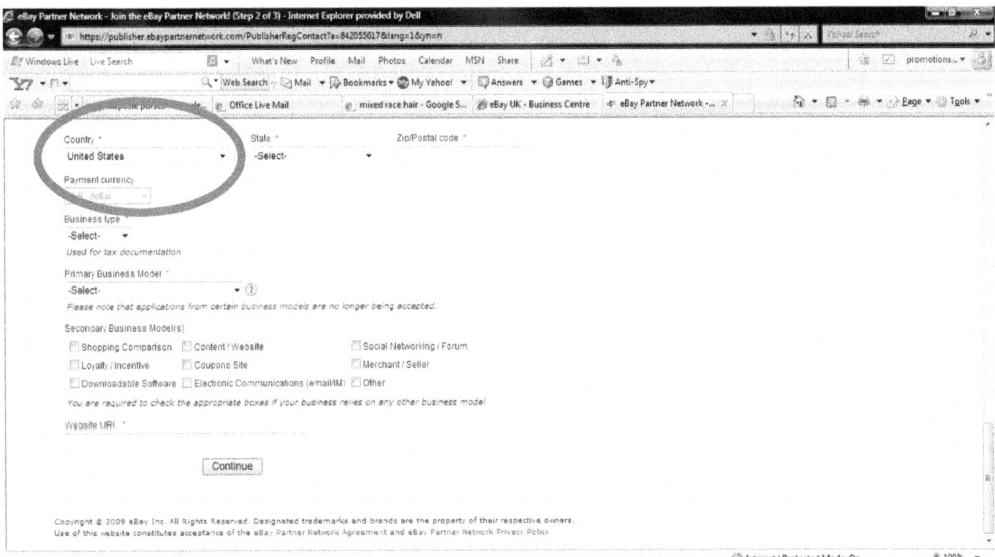

- Be sure to select all the correct options on the form. For example, the name of country and currency. You will also be asked to confirm how you would like to be paid and confirm that you are not a US tax payer. eBay will email you at the email address you stated on the registration form, click on the link that you received in the email from eBay, enter your password and your affiliate account will be activated.

- The "Dashboard" screen (below) will appear. This is where you can view the number of times your advertising link(s) will be clicked and the amount you have earned. The other tabs will allow you to make changes/ updates.

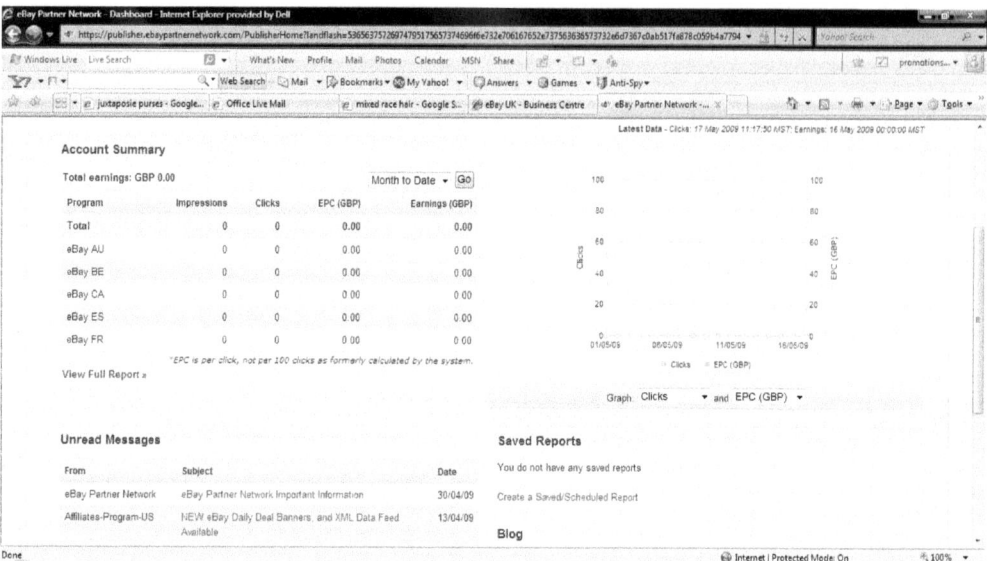

How to create a campaign on eBay

A campaign number is a tracking number that eBay uses to track your affiliate commissions that you make from each advertising campaign that you host in partnership with them. THIS CAMPAIGN NUMBER IS VERY IMPORTANT. To create a campaign number:

- On the Dashboard screen, click on the "Campaigns" tab marked as K.

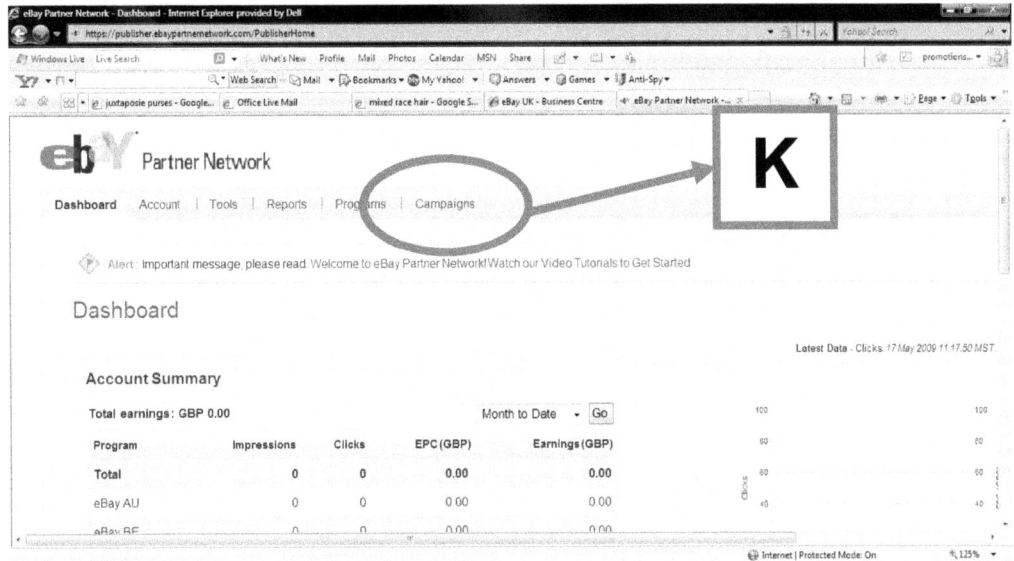

- The screen below will appear when you click on the link "Create Campaign" marked as L below.

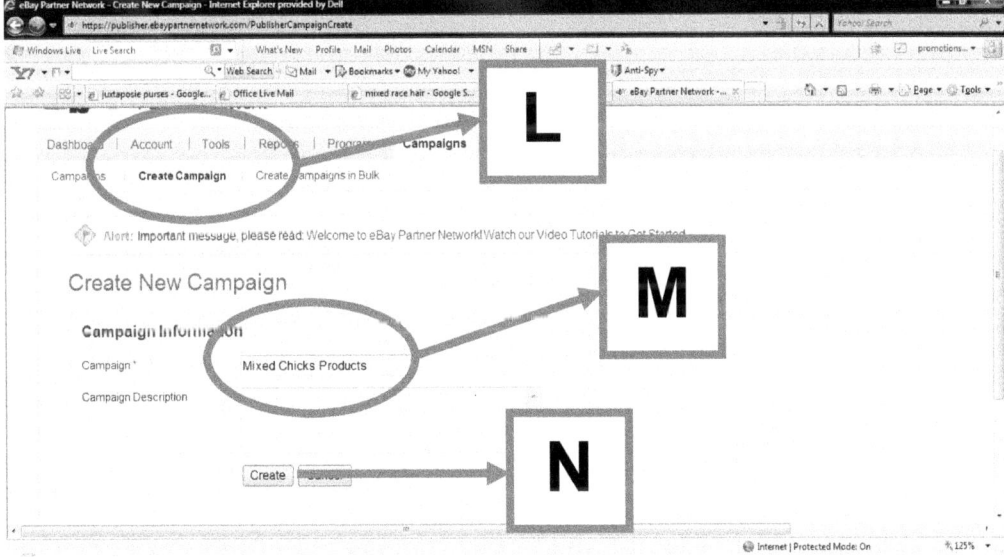

- Next, type in the name of what you want your campaign to be called. If it makes sense to you, you can name campaigns that are the same as the search terms that you used for your keyword search back in chapter 3. For example, I named my campaign "Mixed Chick Products" (marked as M) rather than naming the campaign by the keywords "Mixed Race Hair." This is because eBay specifically have "Mixed Chicks" products for mixed race hair available to purchase.

- Once you decide what to name your campaign, you can click on the "Create" button marked as N (above). You do not have to complete the "Campaign Description" box.

- On the Campaigns tab/ screen, you will see that your campaign has been created marked as O. See below:

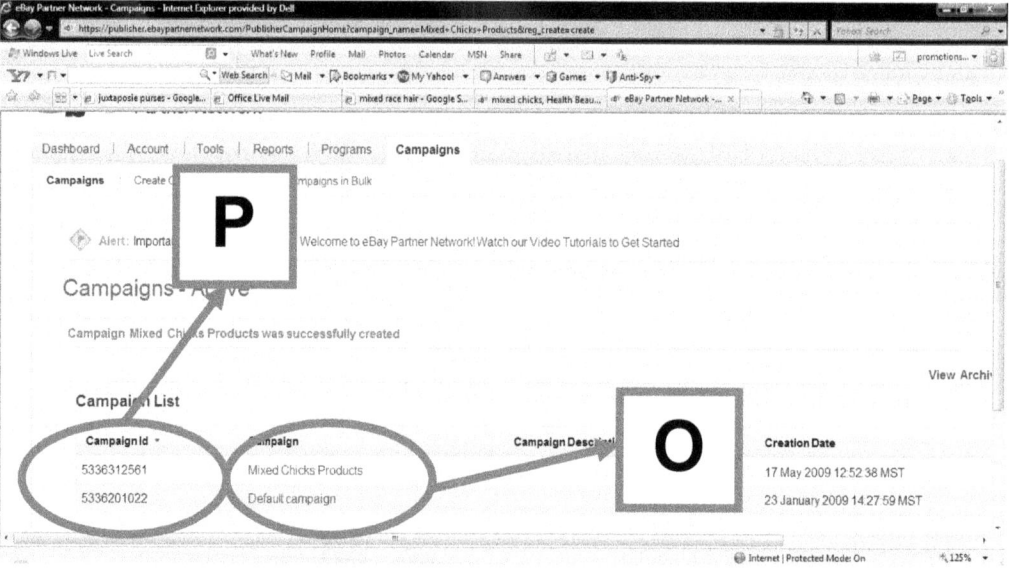

- You now need to copy the campaign ID number of your campaign (marked as P), so that you can insert it into a box when you create your eBay link.

- Click on the "Tools" tab at the top of the screen (marked as Q below) and the screen below will appear. Next click on the "Widgets" button marked as R.

62

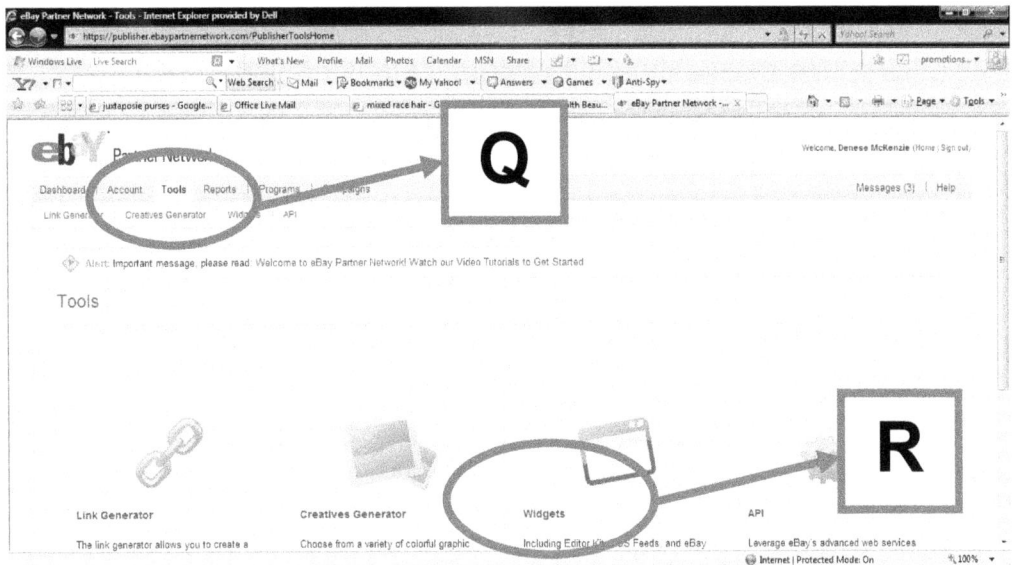

- The page below will appear. In the "Editor kit" column, select eBay UK from the drop down menu (the default option will show as eBay AU) and then click on the "Go" button marked as S below:

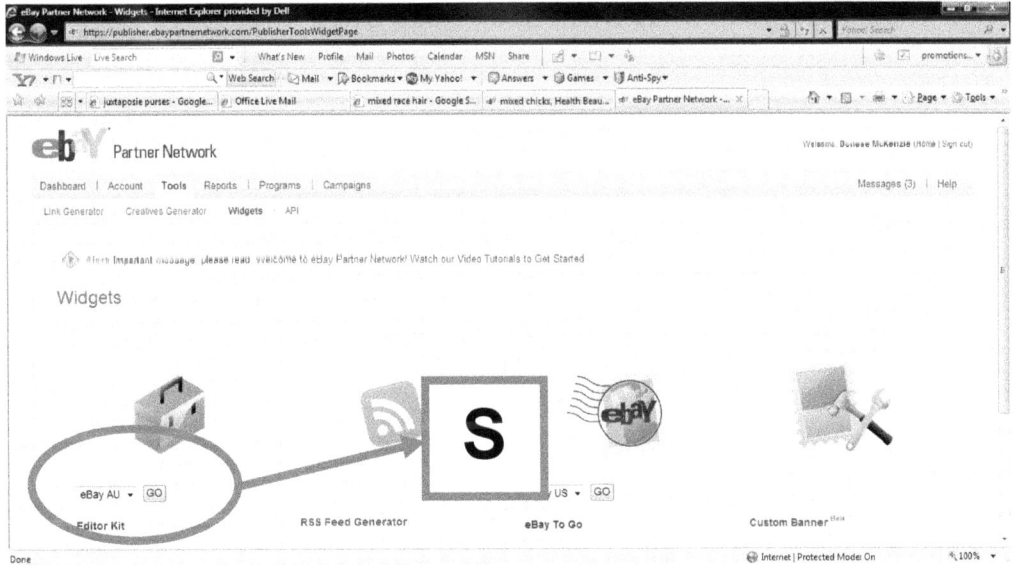

- The pop-up screen below will appear asking you to either register or sign in using your username and password.

63

TIP – You have to create an eBay ID account so that you can trade or sell. Click on the register button to the left of the pop-up screen that appears.

- The form below will appear. Complete the required details – similar to the details you provided when you completed the affiliate programme form.

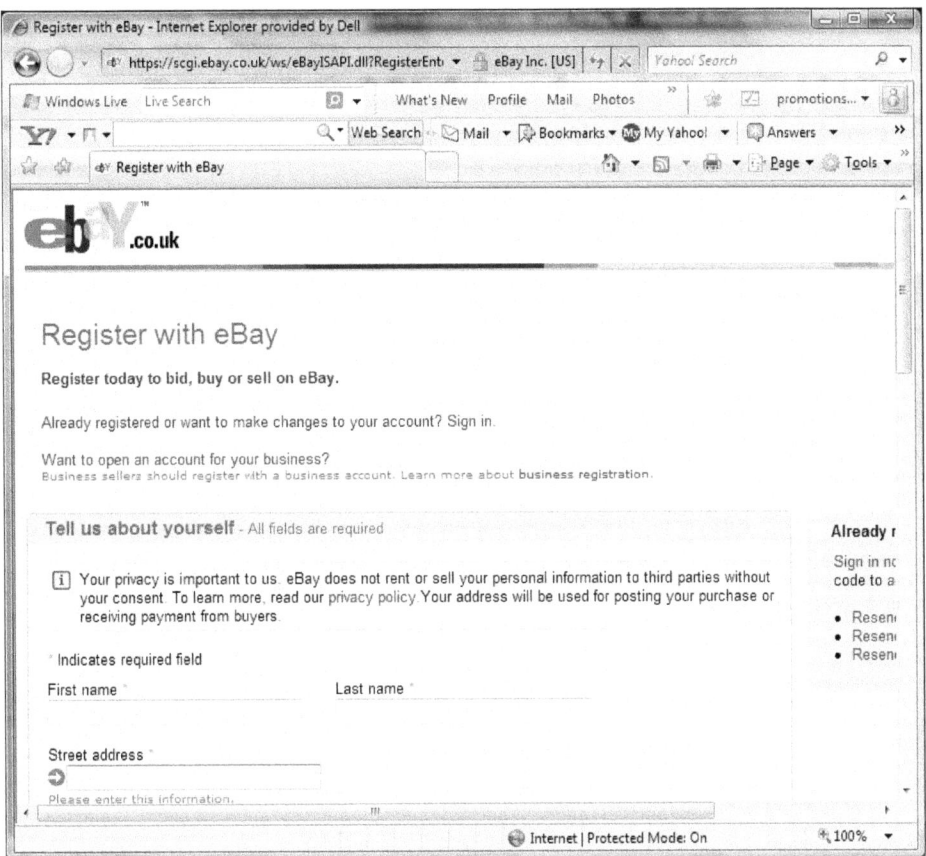

- After you have created your eBay ID to be able to sell/ receive commission credits for your eBay list(s) of products that you want to promote, the screen below will appear. You have to activate your account by going to your email address and clicking on the "Confirm Now" button in the email from eBay.

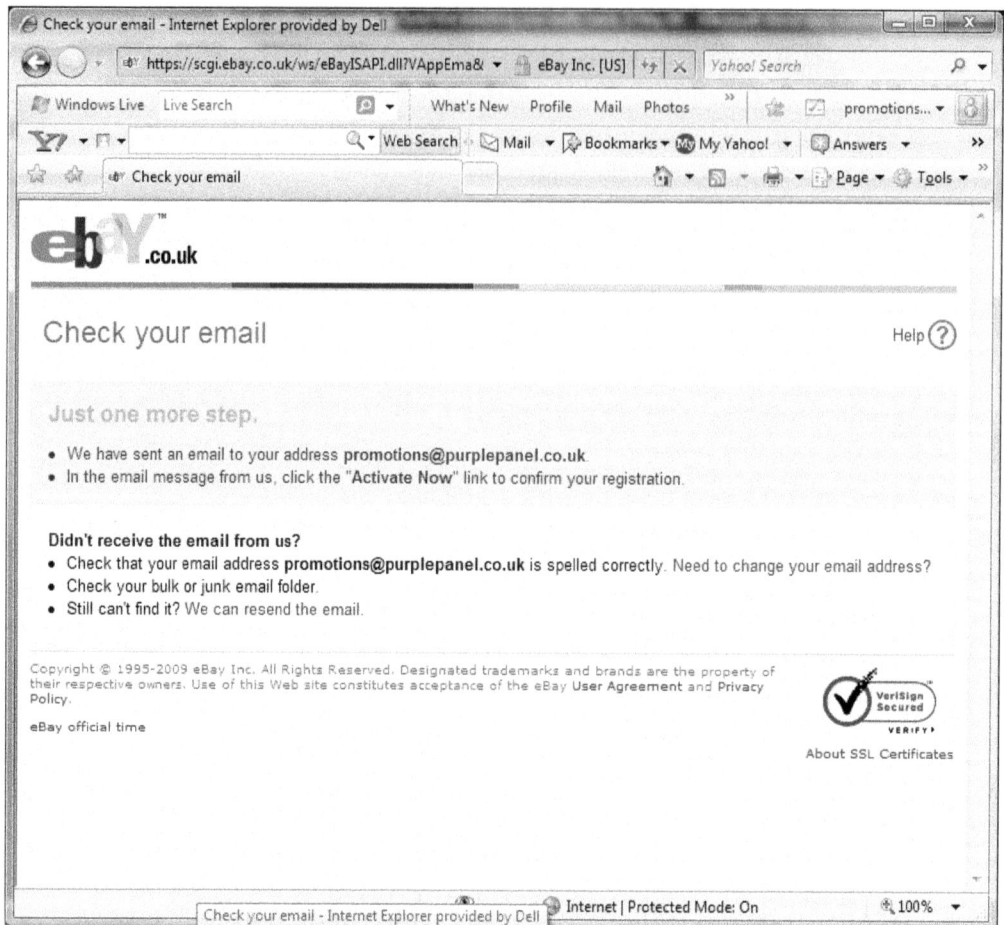

Continuing the process...

- Go back to your affiliate account (you should still be signed in, unless you logged out for some reason) and go back to the "Tools" tab to see the screen below:

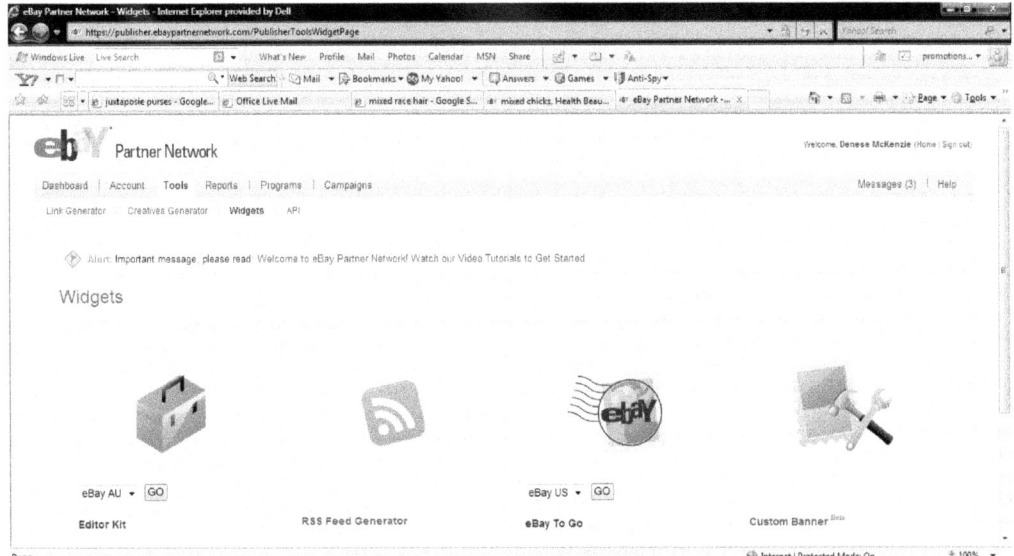

- This time, when the screen below pops up after you select "eBay UK" from the drop down menu in the Editor Kit and click the "GO" button, sign in using your new eBay member profile linked specifically for your advertising/ promotion campaigns (marked as S1):

- After you sign into eBay Editor Kit, it will ask you to confirm your agreement to eBay's license agreement. Once you agree to the terms and conditions, the following screen will appear – taking you to the Editor Kit:

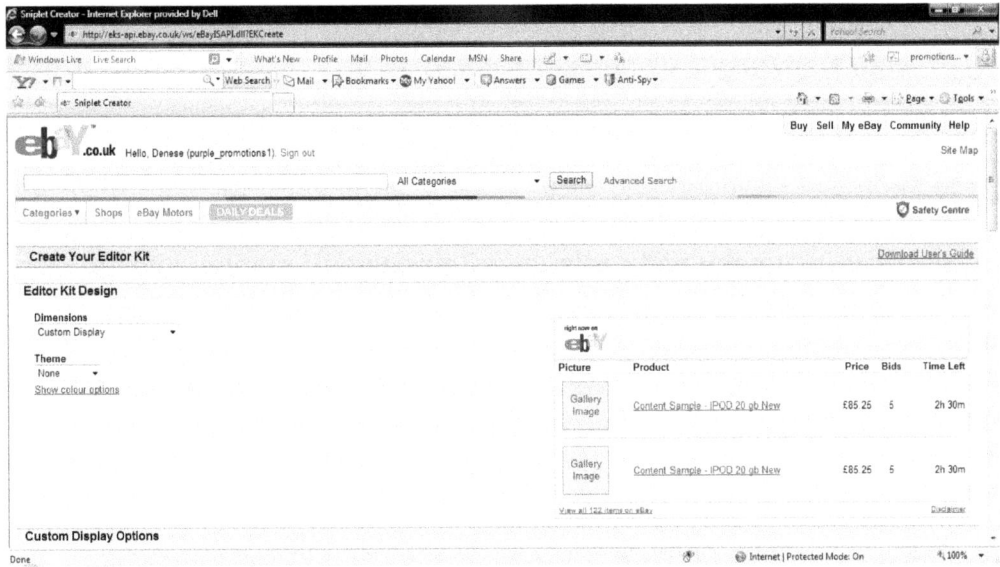

- You can keep the settings as they are – i.e. the display options of the lists. As you scroll down the page, you can add any keywords marked as T below:

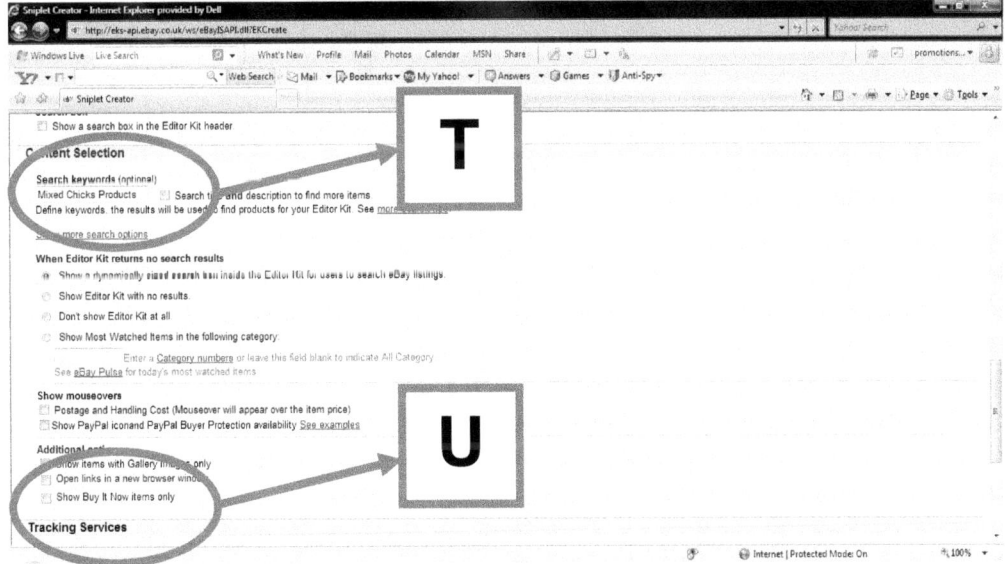

- Under the Tracking Services option (marked U), on the drop down menu named "Provider", select the "eBay Partner Network" option.

69

- Directly underneath the Provider option, the form will ask you for your Campaigns ID number marked as V.

TIP - Remember, you can find the ID number for your campaign if you go to the top of the page and click on the "Campaigns" tab.

- Type in or copy and paste your Campaign ID number into the box marked as V.

- In the Custom ID field you can type in the name of the campaign. In this example, I named my campaign "Mixed Chicks Products." Once you are happy with what you have entered, click "Continue."

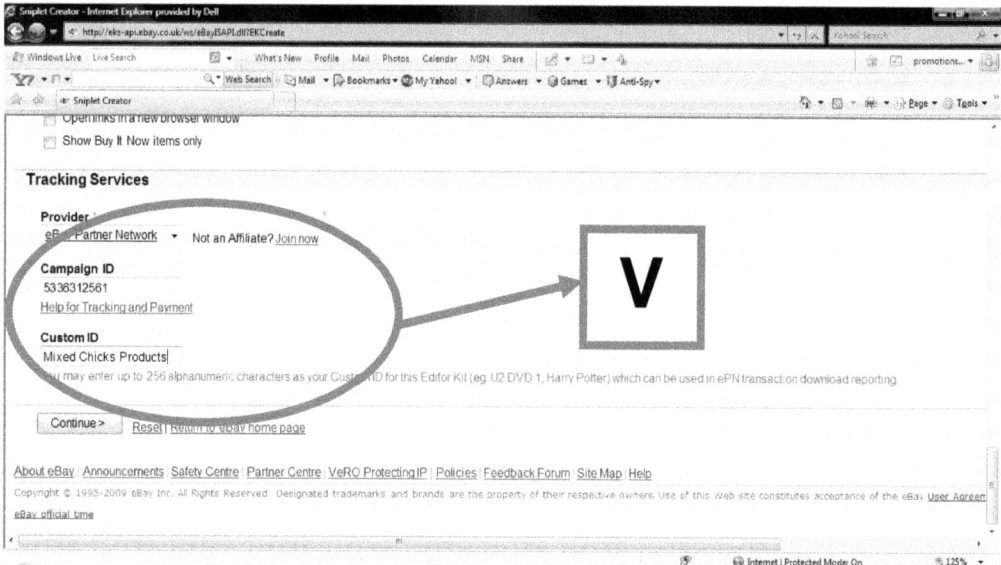

- The page below will appear. It will display the code (marked as V1) that you need to insert into your website as HTML code. This will be covered shortly regarding how to do this.

TIP – Ensure that you scroll down and check that the preview of the listings, display the most relevant products.

- You can go back and review changes to keywords marked as V2. If you go back and review the keywords that you entered before, you can increase the number of items on the listing or create a more varied or more specific list.

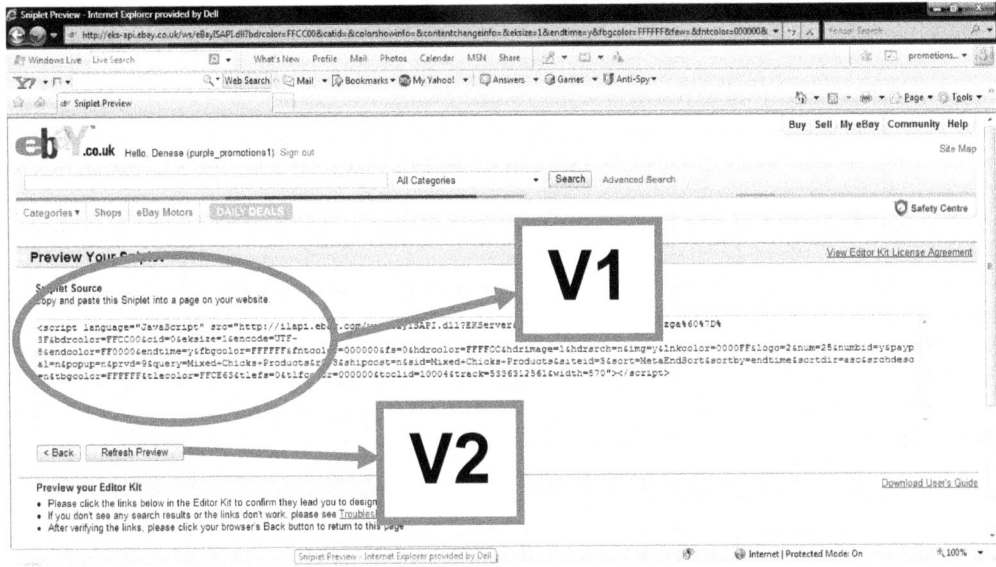

- The next screen shows how the listings will be displayed marked as W.

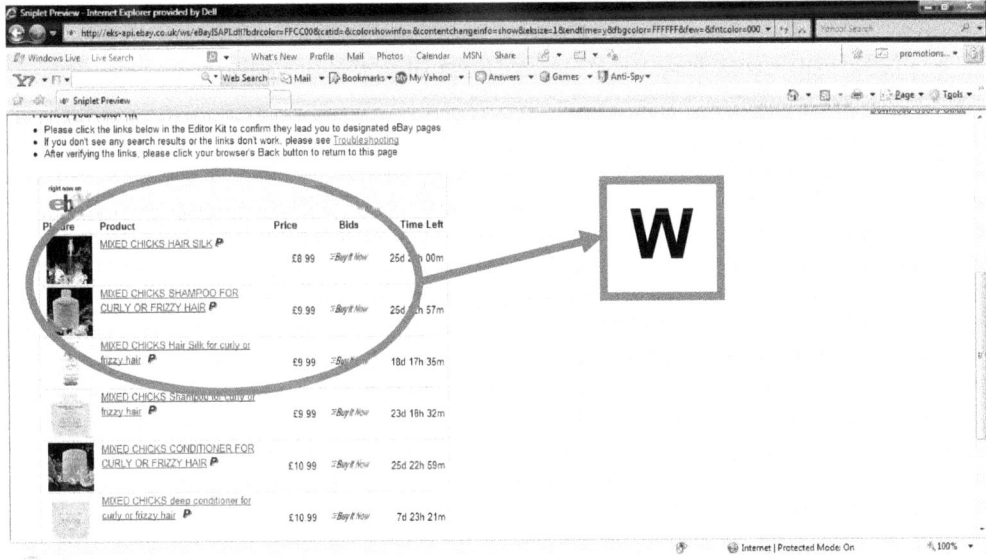

- Once you are happy with the listings, you need to copy the "Sniplet Source" code into your website.

- To copy the code, place your mouse cursor at point X (i.e. at the end of the code) and then press the function keys "Ctrl" and "A" on your keyboard. Then right click on your mouse and select the "Copy" option on the pop-up box to copy the code – ready to paste into your website.

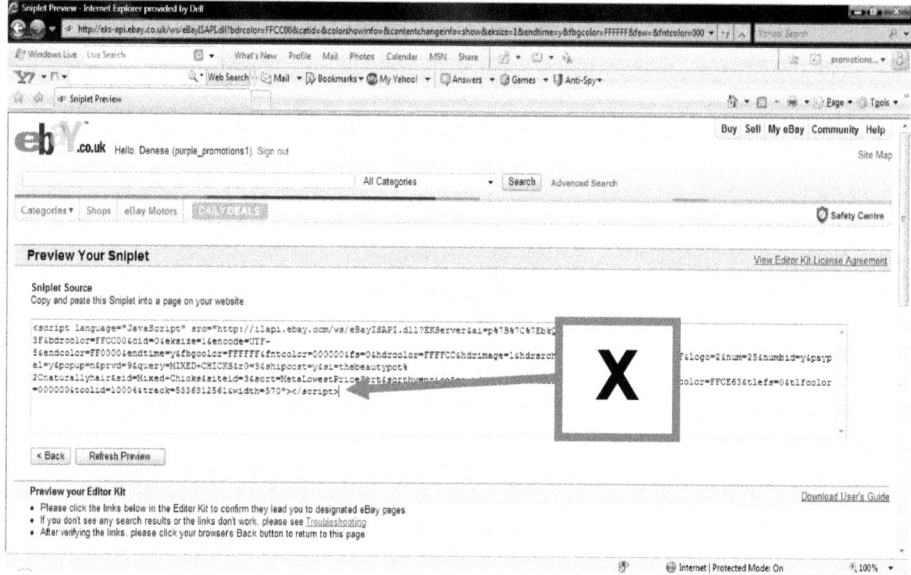

- Next, go back to your free website at www.weebly.com that you created earlier.

- Once you are logged in, click on the "Edit site" link. The home page of your website will appear under the "Elements" tab.

- Click and drag the "Custom HTML" element (marked as Y) onto the page and/ or position that you want.

- For this example, I wanted my e-bay listing on the "Hair Care products" page of my website.

- Once you drag this Custom HTML box onto the page and position you want, click on "Edit Custom HTML" marked as Z and then paste the Sniplet code from eBay into the space on your page.

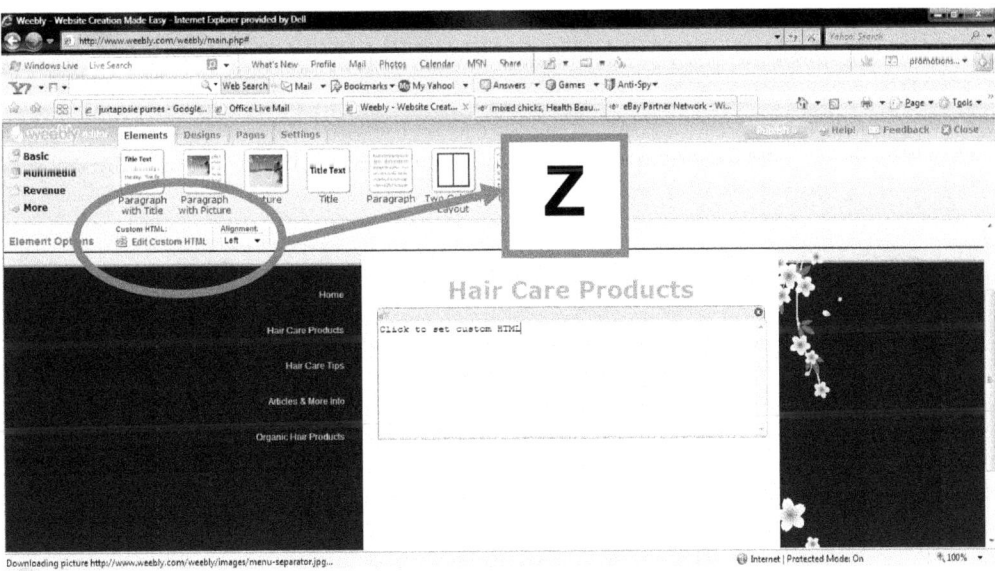

- The code will appear at first and then your eBay listing will appear on your website page. See below. Click on the "Publish button to make your eBay listings live marked as Z1.

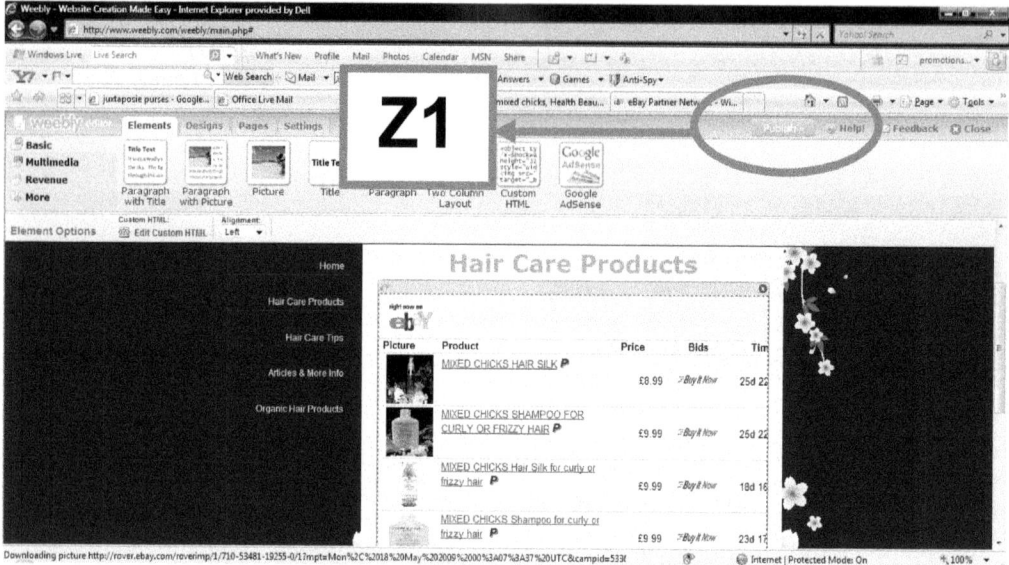

- Now your eBay listing will be made available online for visitors to your site to bid on or purchase. Each time a product is purchased via the link on your website, you will be paid a commission.

Chapter 6 - How to advertise the products and services you want to promote

To re-cap from the previous chapter, so far you have:

- Registered an affiliate account in eBay.

- Created your first campaign on eBay, which included an "Editor Kit" account

- Enhanced your first website (dedicated to online income) by posting your first live, eBay campaign to promote your selected products/ services.

Using Google Adwords to generate the income you want

- First of all, please visit www.google.co.uk and click on the link "Advertising programmes" marked as A below:

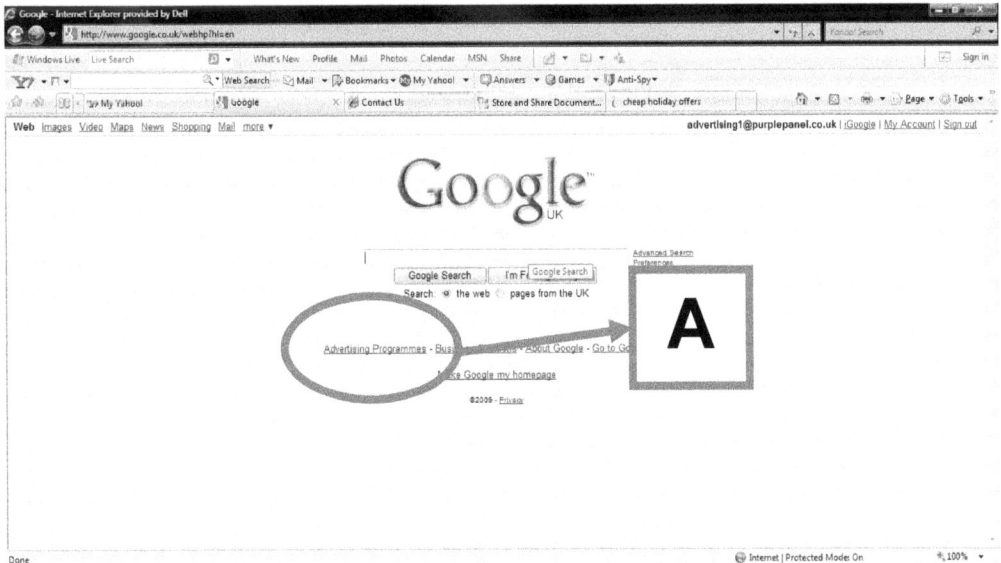

- The page below will appear. Click on the Google Adwords link marked as B:

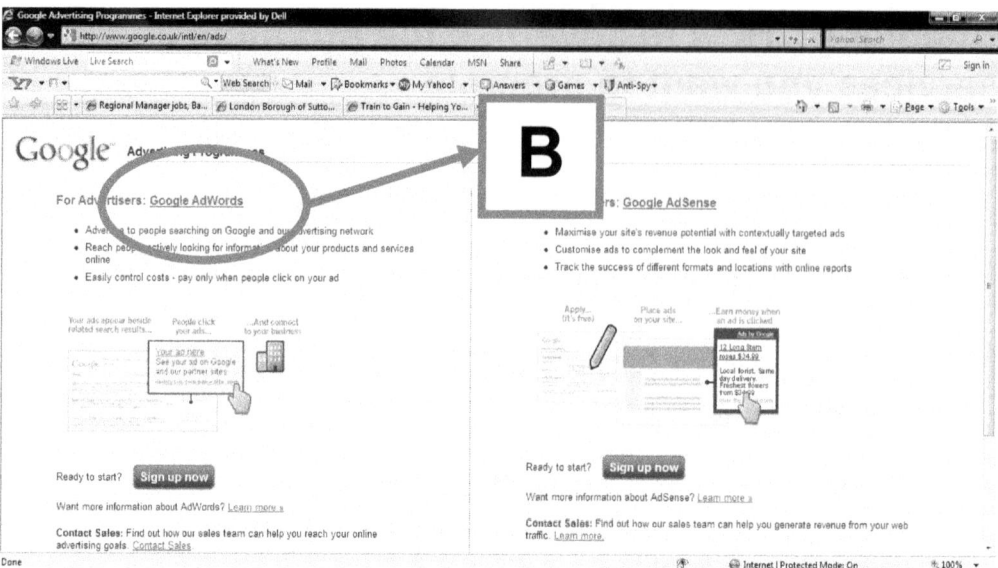

- The page below will appear. Once you click on the "Try Adwords now" button (marked as C), you will be taken to another page.

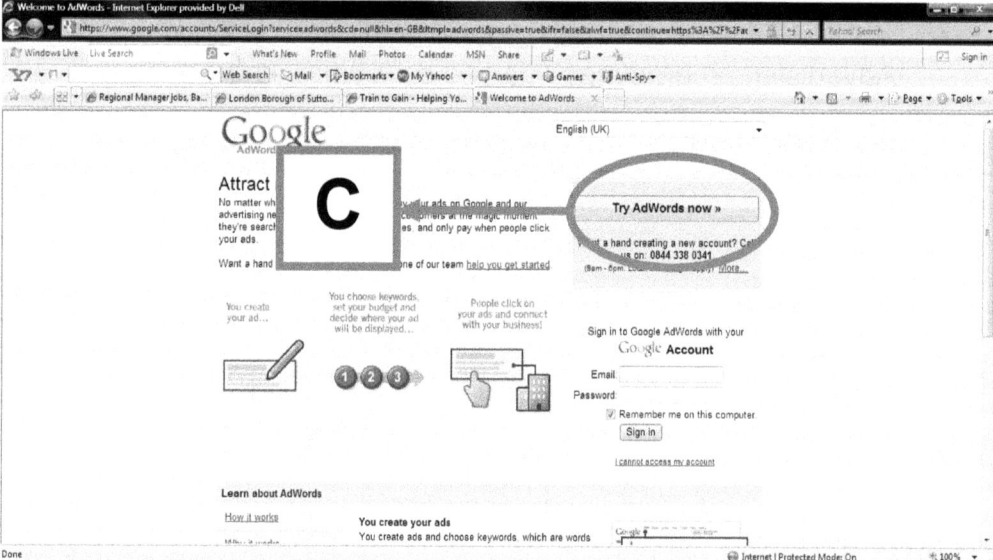

- You will have the option of creating 2 types of accounts. Select the "Standard Edition" account option marked as D below and click on the "Continue" button.

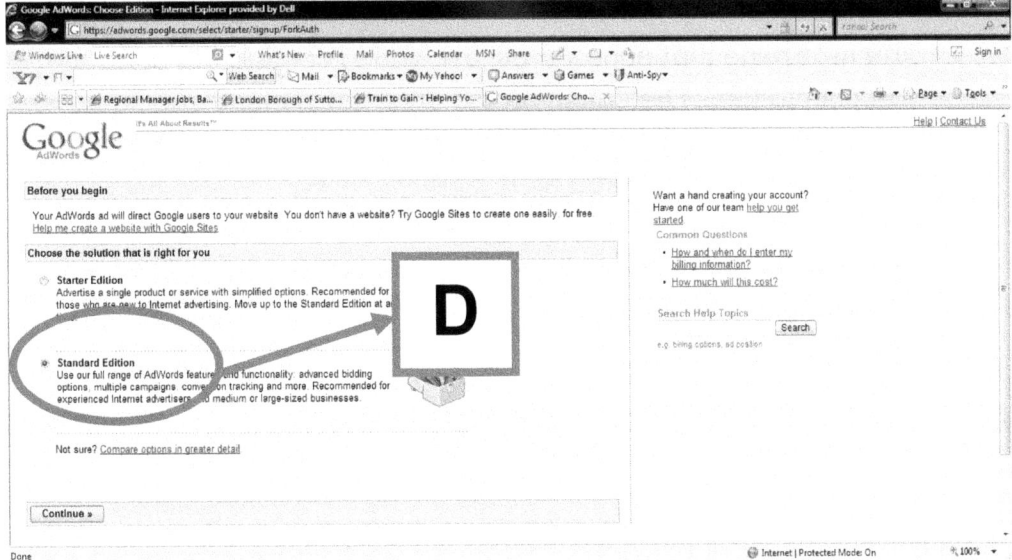

- You will be asked to log a username and password.

TIP – Remember the dedicated email address that you created earlier? Use this to create a username for your account. You also need to log into your email account to verify and activate your Google account.

- Once you complete your details, scroll down this page and click on the "Create an account" button.

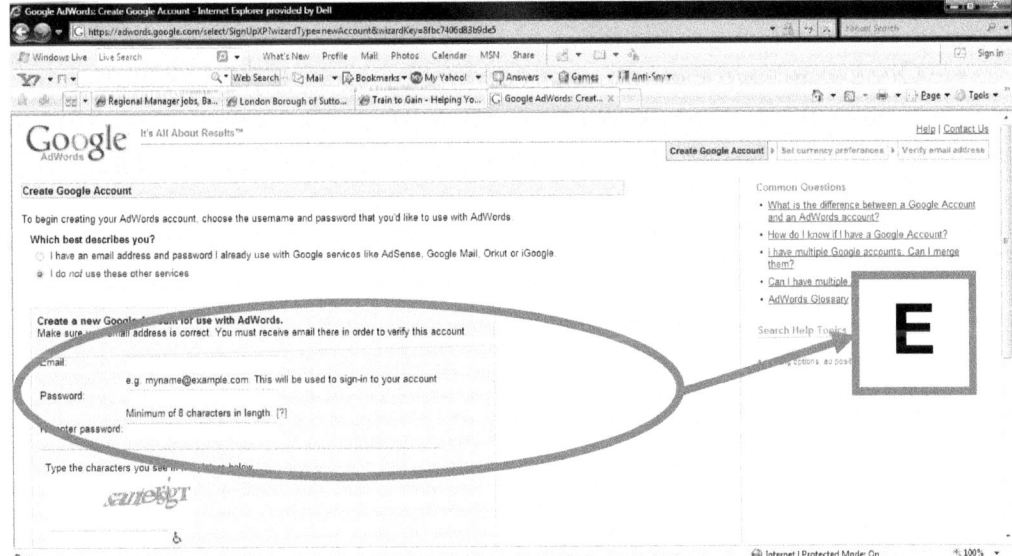

- The next page that appears will ask you to confirm the currency you plan to use. The option on the drop down menu should be defaulted to "British Pounds Sterling." Once checked, click on the "Continue button" marked as F.

- Next you will be asked to log into your email account to verify your new Google Adwords account. YOU MUST DO THIS BEFORE YOU CONTINUE.

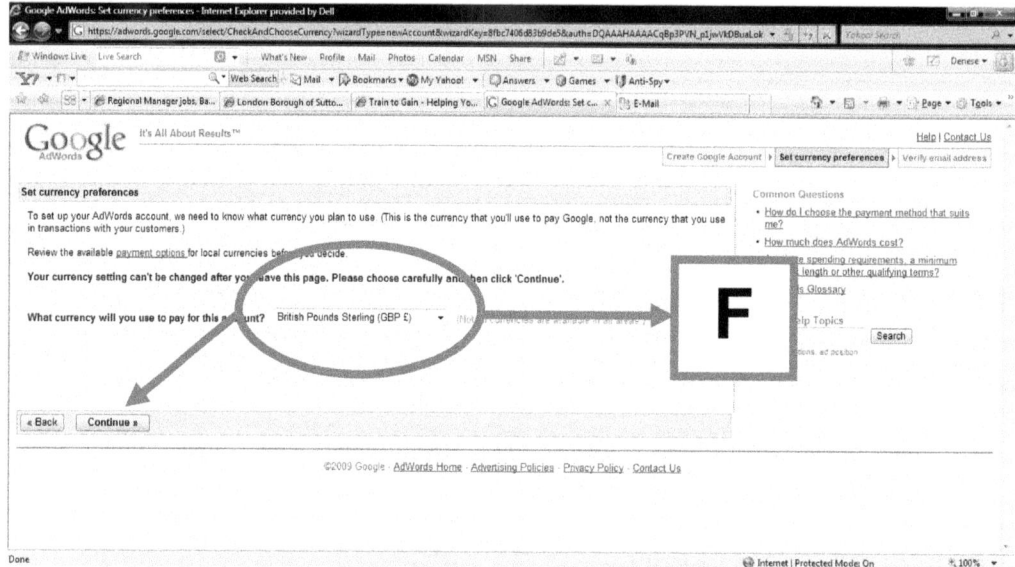

- Once you have verified your account by clicking the link sent in the email sent by Google to your dedicated email account, the page below will appear. Click on the link marked G to start creating your advert.

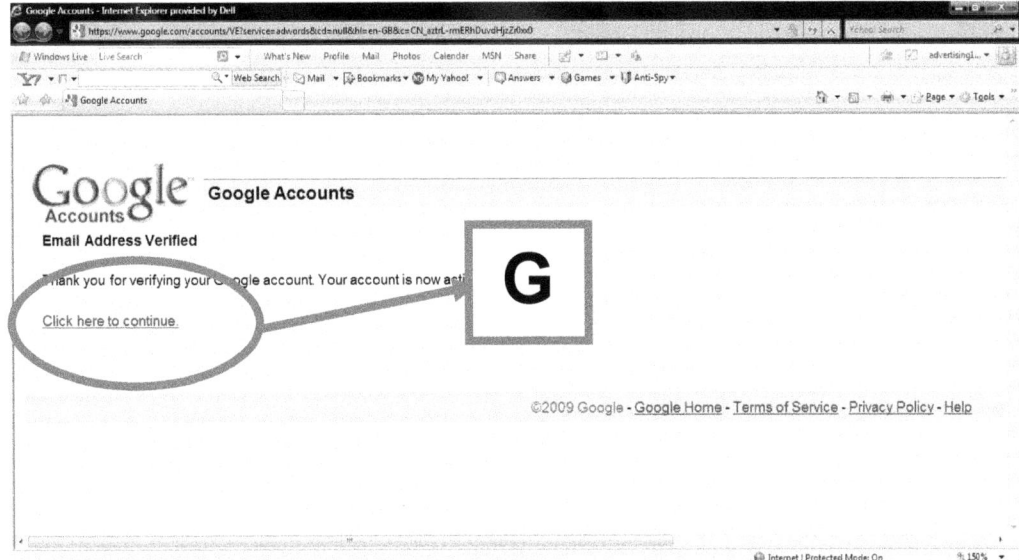

- When the page below appears, click on the "Create your campaign" button marked as H.

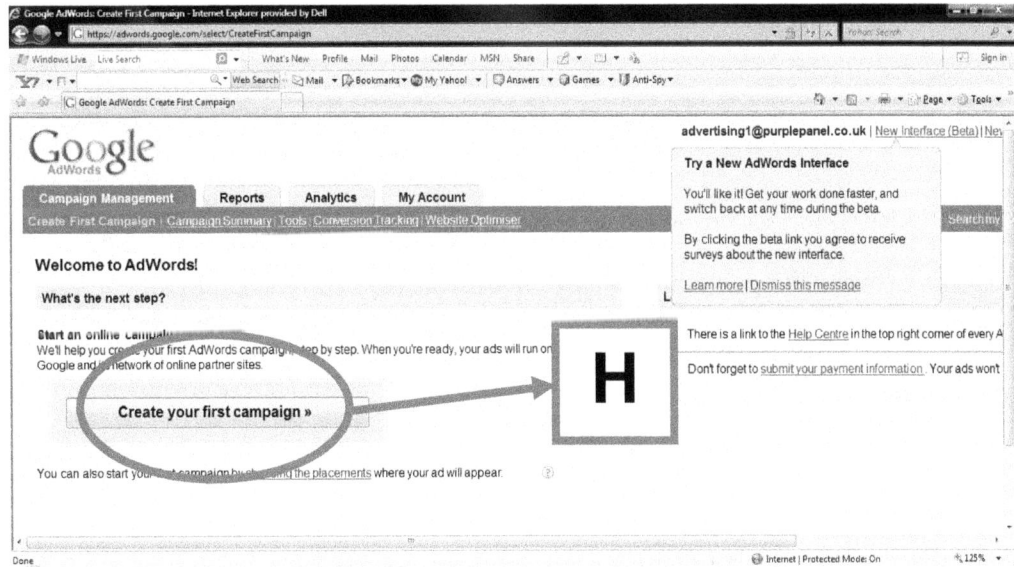

TIP – You may find that Google takes you to the page below rather than connecting you straight through to the above page. You can sign into your Google account in the login box marked as I below.

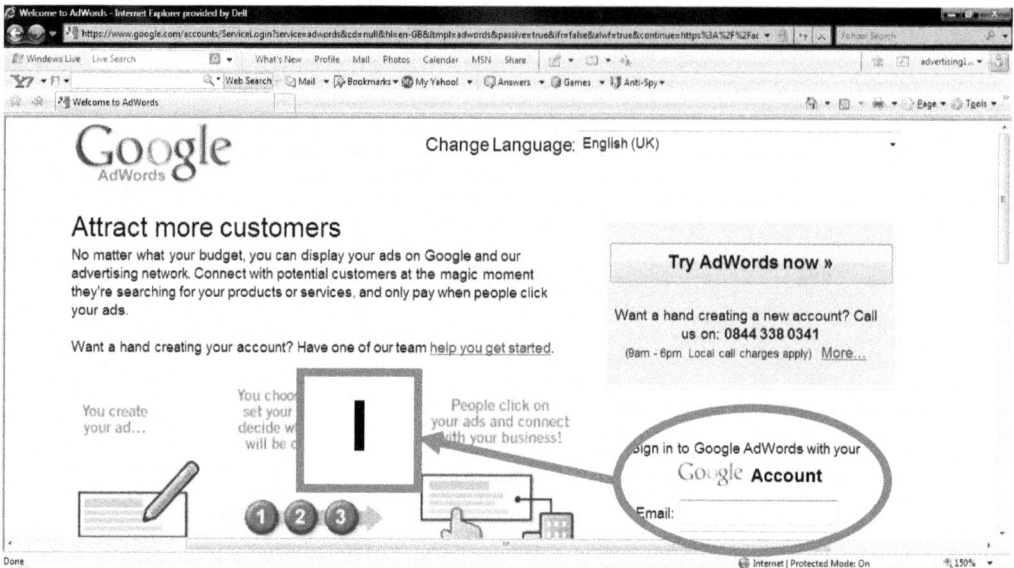

- Once you click on the "Create your first campaign" button, you will be taken to the "Welcome" page below. Scroll down and check the details and click on the "Continue" button.

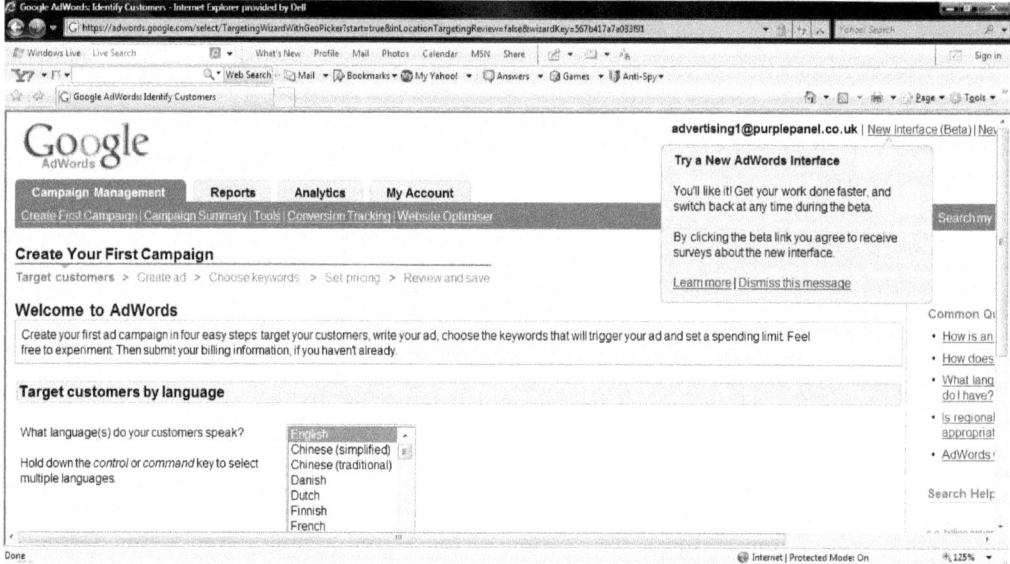

- The page below will appear where you will have to enter the text for your first advert.

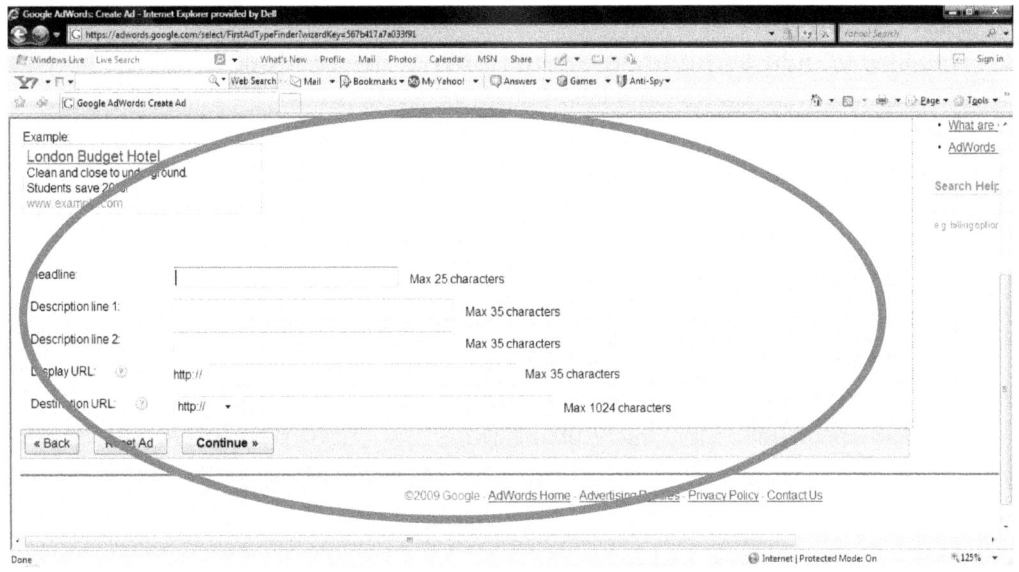

Writing your first Google Adwords advert

Before completing the form in Google for your first advert, a draft advert must be written first using the keywords you identified earlier for your chosen product/ service. By using my example of promoting hair products for mixed race hair, the following keywords were identified:

- Mixed race hair
- Shampoo
- Conditioner
- Hair care products
- Hair care

The basic structure of the form in Google can be used to help you draft your first advert. The core elements of an advert include the following:

THE HEADLINE
This must include the keywords you identified previously.

Description (line 1)
This line should give people or searchers summarised information that they need, for example the price of a product/ service or the amount of a product that is available.

Description (line 2)
This line should summarise the benefits of the product or service

Destination
This line should state the URL – i.e. the address of your website that you created earlier.

> **TIP** – Creating adverts by using Google is a cost effective way of marketing and testing what works the best to promote your website link that you have created to promote your selected products or services. Testing your adverts in this way is more immediate and you can monitor and track how many times potential customers have clicked on your adverts to use and purchase the products or services you have chosen to promote.

The content that you add in Description lines 1 and 2, can offer you the flexibility you need to target different searchers. The searchers that I decided to target for my example of promoting products for mixed race hair include:

- Professional women who have mixed race hair
- Parents of mixed raced children
- Teenagers with mixed race hair

Using the basic structure of an advert, the table below shows what an advert aimed at professional women could look like for my example:

	Identified keywords: Mixed race hair, shampoo, conditioner, hair products, hair care
	Advert example:
Headline	Mixed race hair products
Description line 1	Shampoos & Conditioners from £9.99
Description line 2	Quality range of products available
Display URL	http://mixedracehair.weebly.com
Target searcher:	Professional women

- Once you are happy with your draft advert, you can return to your Google account to enter your advert. When you are happy with what you have entered, scroll down the page and click the continue button.

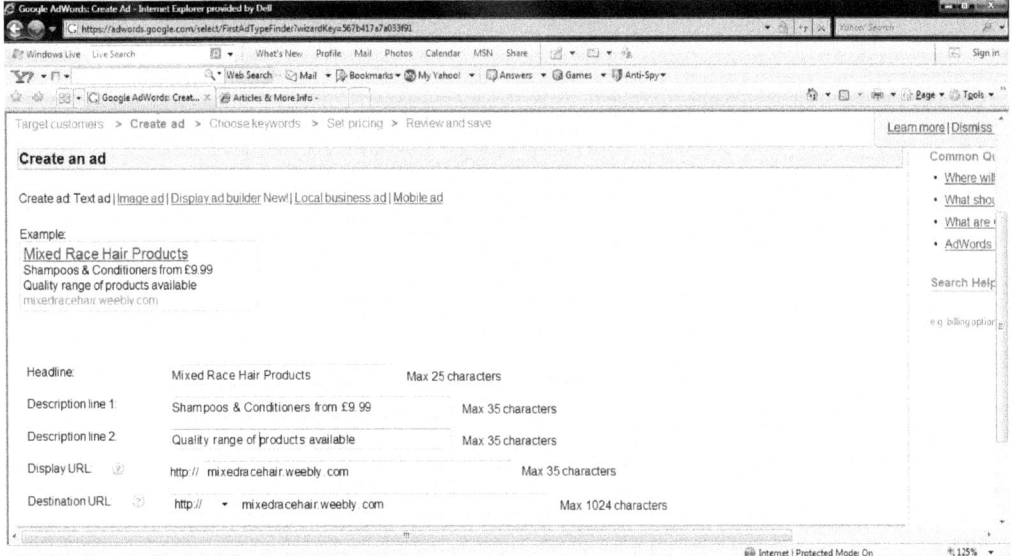

- The page below will appear. Add the keywords that you want to use. For my example, I used the keywords I identified previously and which I used in the advert.

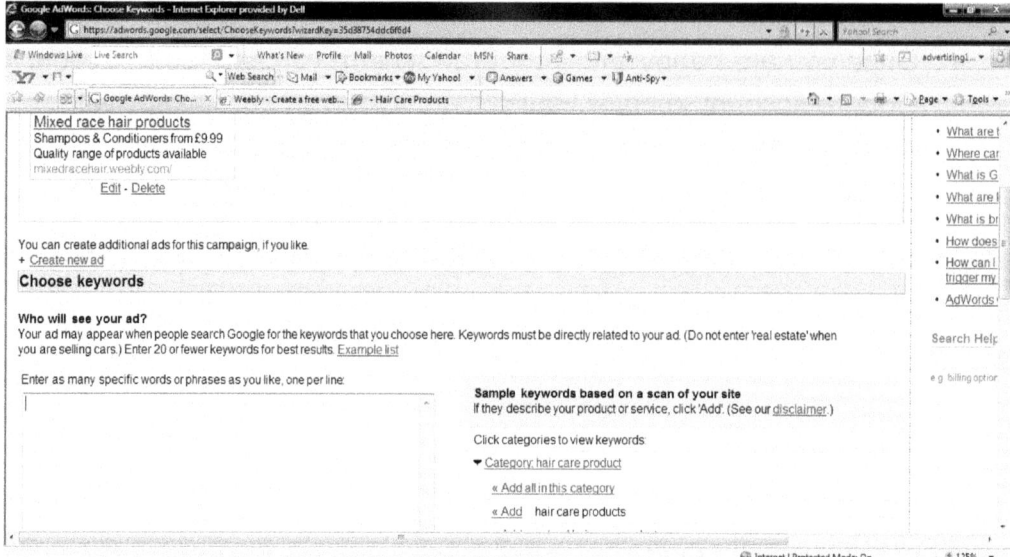

- In the space marked as J, add your keywords. Google will also give suggested keywords for you to add based on their results after they have scanned the main content of your website.

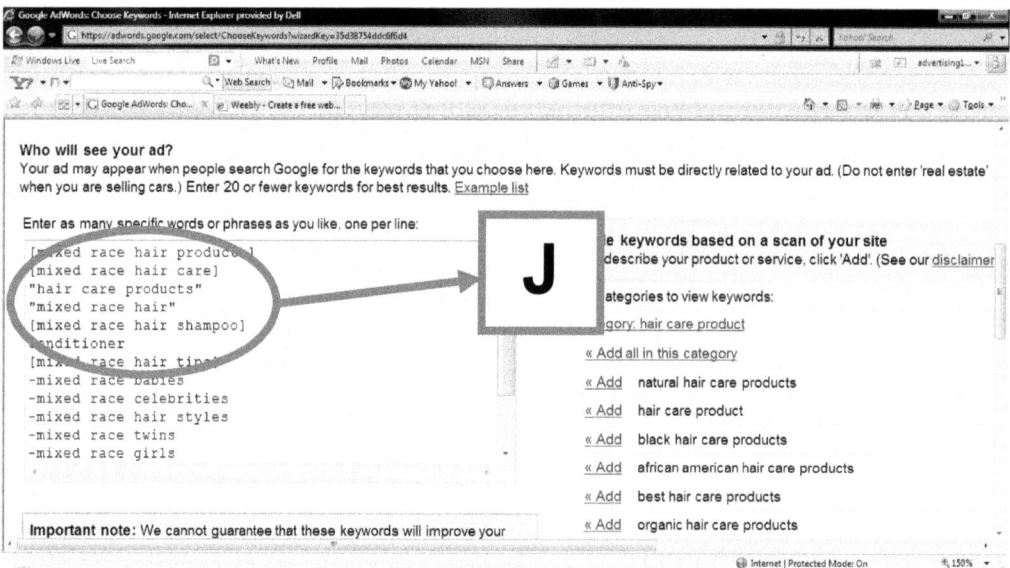

TIP – You will notice that some keywords I entered for this example have different signs or brackets. To explain I'll use the keyword Mixed Hair for this example:

Broad match - When you enter your keyword like this – e.g. Mixed Hair, this allows your advert to show for searches on similar phrases and relevant variations.

Phrase match – When you enter your keyword like this – e.g. "Mixed Hair", this allows your advert to show for searches that match the exact phrase.

Exact match – When you enter your keyword like this – e.g. [Mixed Hair], this allows your advert to appear for searches that match the exact term only.

Negative match – When you enter your keyword like this – e.g. –Mixed Hair, this ensures that your advert is not shown for any searches that include this keyword or term.

Once you are happy with the keywords that you have entered, scroll down to the end of the page and click the "continue" button. The page below will appear:

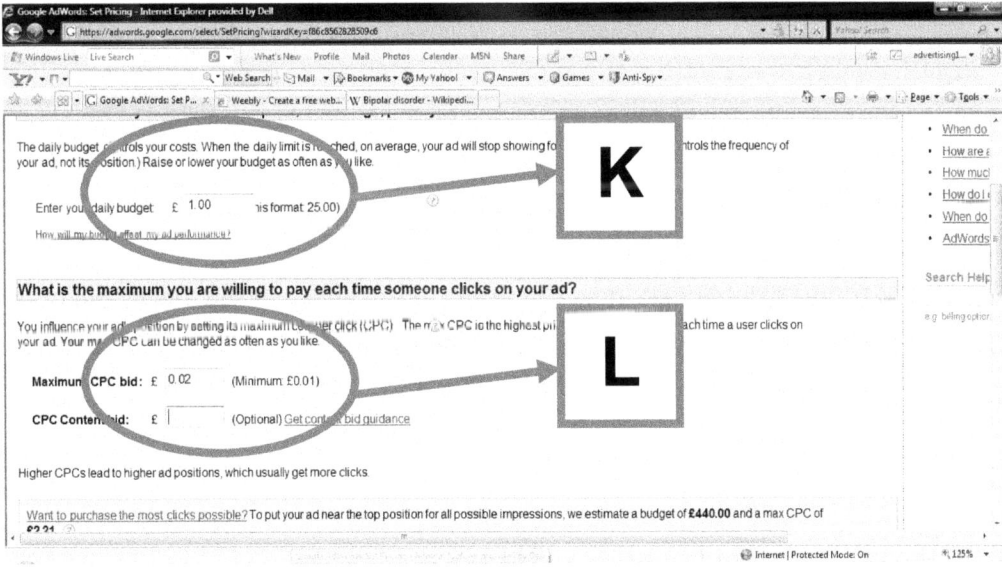

- Enter the daily budget that you are willing to pay per day to cover the costs whenever a searcher clicks on your advert link marked as K.

- Also enter how much you want to pay for each time a searcher clicks on your advert marked L. You can change the details of your campaign and daily budget at any time. You can also place your campaign on pause at any time.

- The page below will appear which gives you the chance to edit any changes before confirming your billing payment method and details.

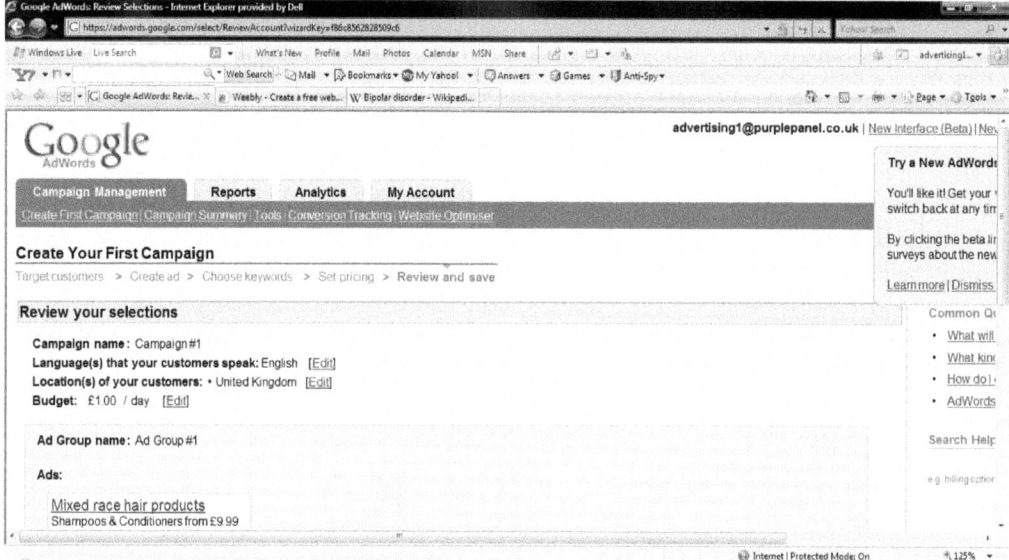

- Next you will be asked to complete your account set-up details, i.e. whether you will be paying by credit card or direct debit each time that a searcher clicks on your advert.

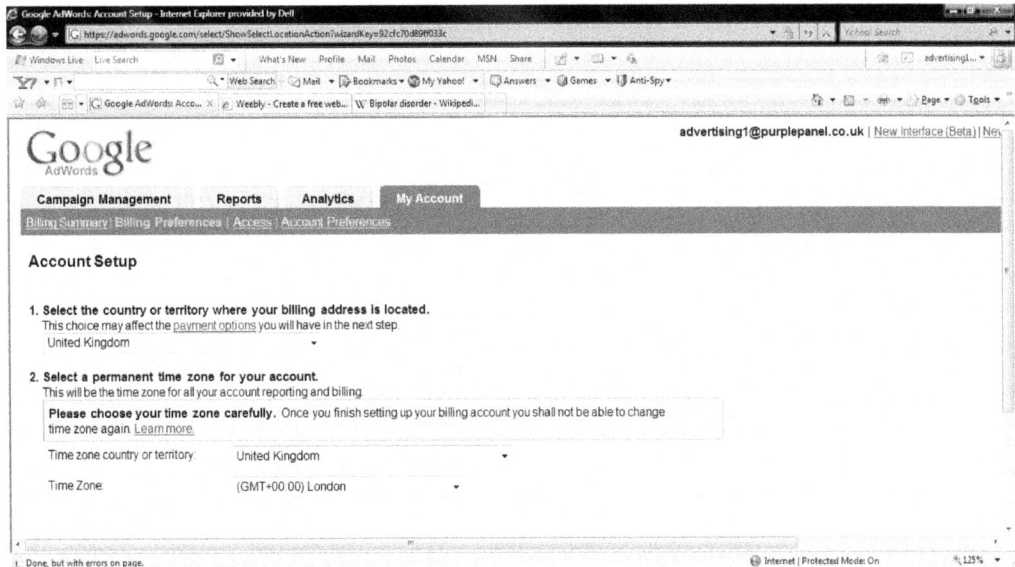

- Once you click the continue button, you will be taken to the page below, asking you to agree to the service terms. Select "Yes" marked as M and click the continue button.

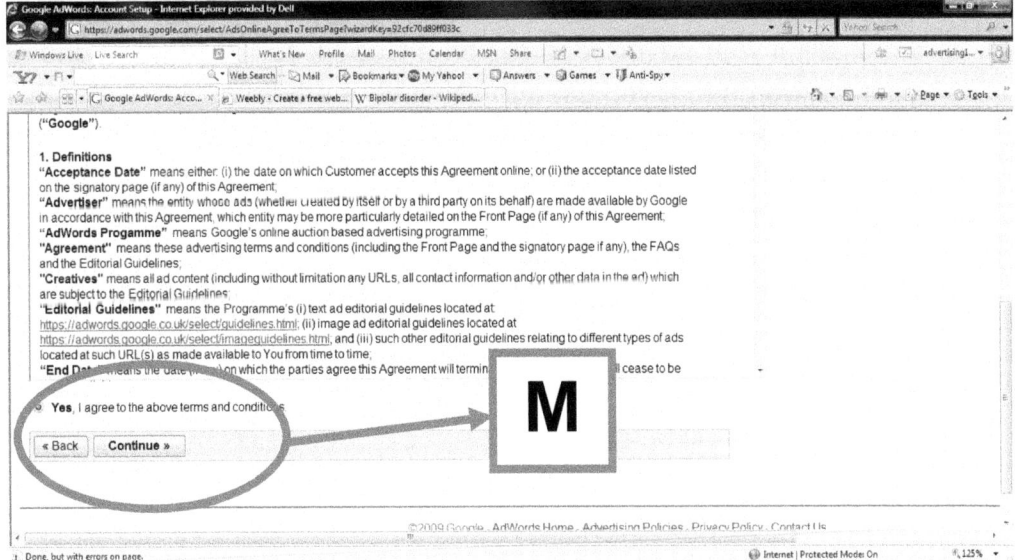

- Once you click "Continue" on this page, you will be asked to complete your credit or debit card details. Once you complete these, click the "Save and activate button" marked as N.

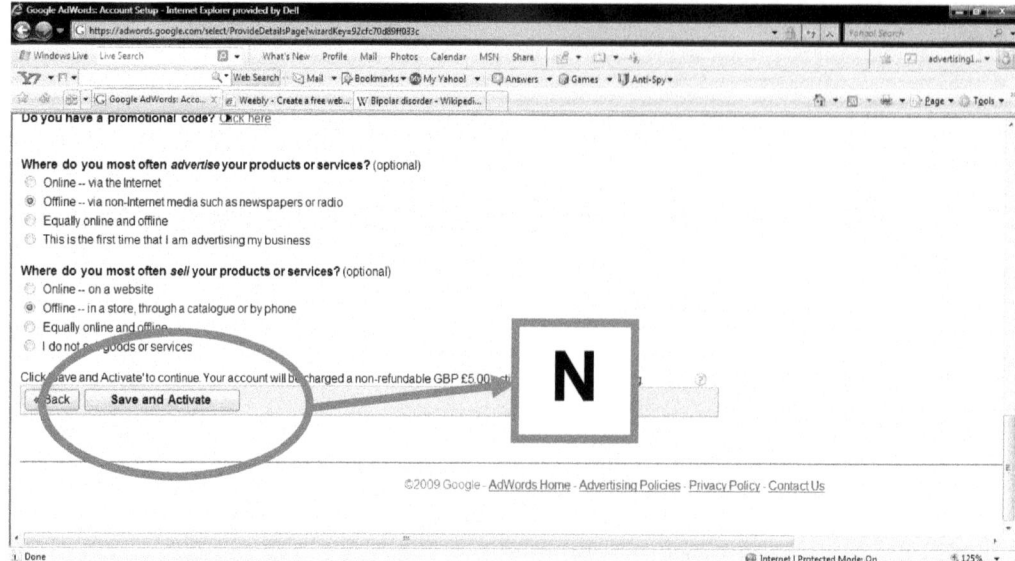

- Once complete, Google will confirm that the set up is completed and that your advert will be featured online shortly.

Checking your advert

- To check if your advert features on a Google search, type in one of your keywords that you used to see if your advert appears. For this example, I searched Google by entering the keywords "mixed race hair care." You will notice that my advert ranks in 2nd position! (Marked as O below).

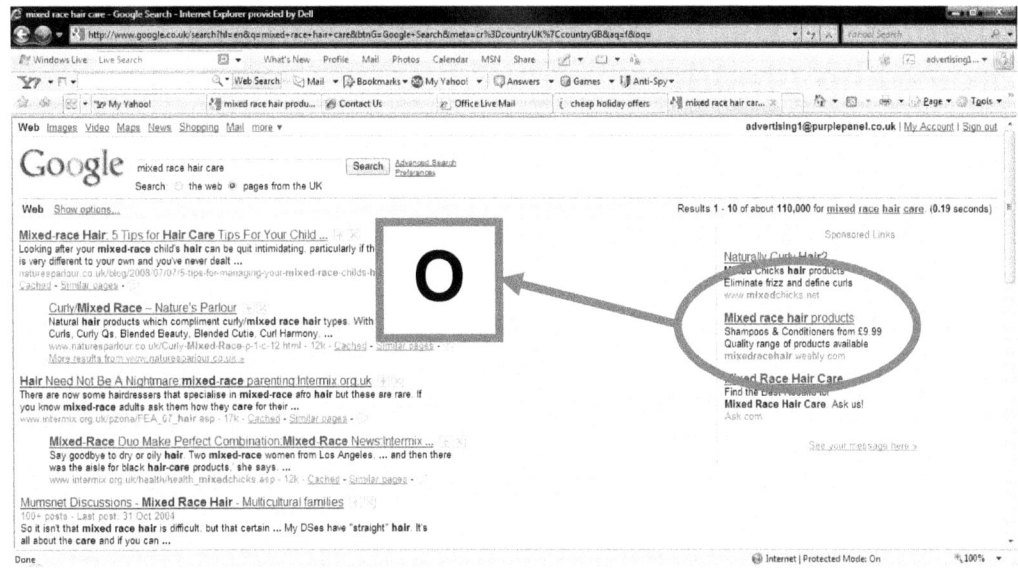

Monitoring and tracking your advert campaign

- If you want to keep track of your advert and its activity, click on the "Campaign Management" tab whenever you are logged into your account.

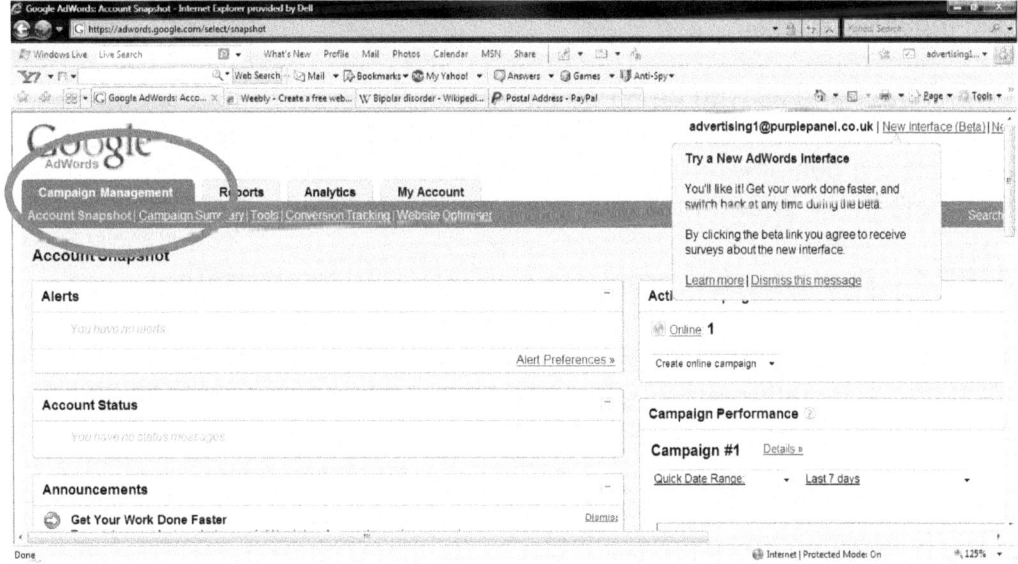

TIP – Don't forget that you can edit and change your advert at anytime. You can also create adverts with different wording to test what adverts work best for your chosen products and services.

Chapter 7 – Using Amazon to make money by promoting products

To re-cap from the previous chapter, so far you have:

- Registered a new Google Adwords account

- You have utilised keywords you identified to draft your first advert

- You have loaded and saved your first Google Adwords advert

- You have set your daily budget and cost per clicks for your advert

- You have completed the billing set-up and viewed your advert

Promoting products on Amazon can be a great way to make money so that you can pay for the wedding that you *really* want.

Amazon has built a strong brand of trust and choice and so most people are likely to purchase products from Amazon, besides purchasing books and music.

One of the benefits with being affiliated with Amazon is that they offer multiple recommendations when a customer buys something. For example if a customer buys a movie on DVD, Amazon may also recommend the soundtrack album for the movie which is available on CD.

STEP 1 – Explore what products are available to promote

You can see what products are available on Amazon by visiting www.amazon.com/gp/new-releases/ . Use this to get some ideas about what types of products you can promote.

TIP – The products that you choose do not have to be linked together you can promote any products that you want to generate income. For the sake of the stage that you are currently at, you may want to remain within the category you started off with. For the sake of this example, I will continue to use products that link to my theme of promoting hair care products.

TIP - I have found from my own experience that targeting products and services that cost over £100 are likely to generate higher commission rates for you. Also, as the number of products that are purchased via your adverts, websites or links increases, the higher your commission percentage increases too.

Alternatively, to get more ideas of what search terms are used to search for various products including recent trends and to possibly help you to identify areas to promote) you can visit Google Trends at http://www.google.com/trends .

- On the homepage, type in the search terms, products or services you are interested in and click on the "Search trends" button marked as A below:

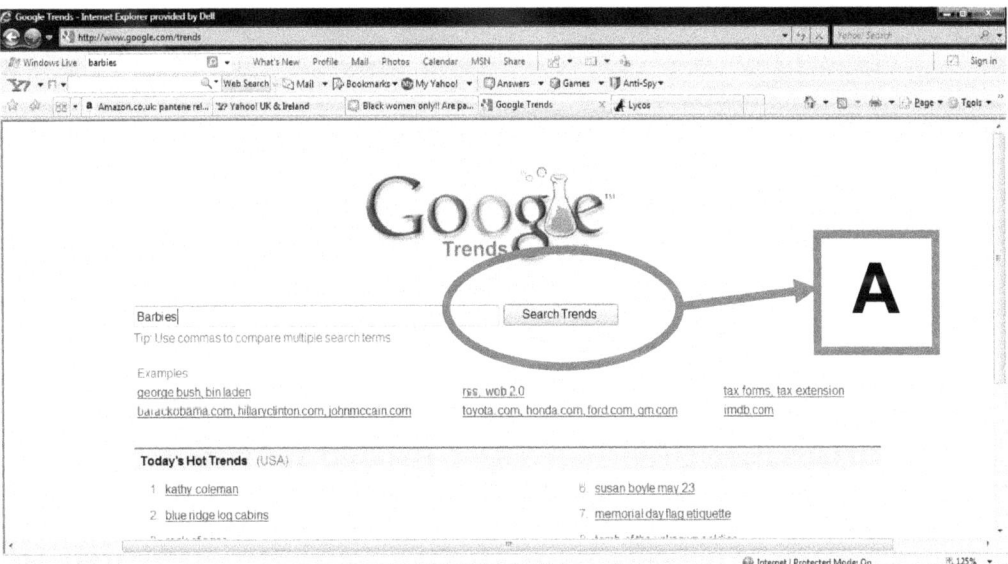

- If there is enough statistics and data available, Google will give you a summary of how much activity these search terms generate. This information is broken down by the activity taking place in different countries.

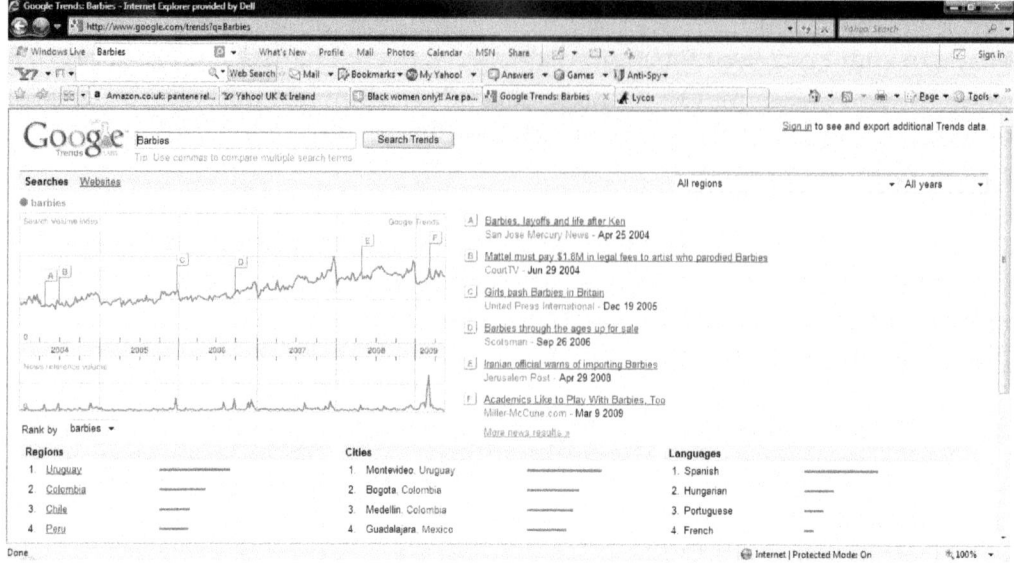

TIP – Knowing what products and/ or services are being searched for in other countries can be useful. This can guide you to promote eBay products in other European countries for example.

- In reference to the main theme/ example that I have used by promoting hair care products, I searched for "Pantene Relaxed and Natural hair care." I found that there was no data available on Google Trends.

- Next, I did a Google search to see if any adverts appeared when I used these search terms "Pantene Relaxed and Natural hair care" - 3 adverts appeared marked as B below.

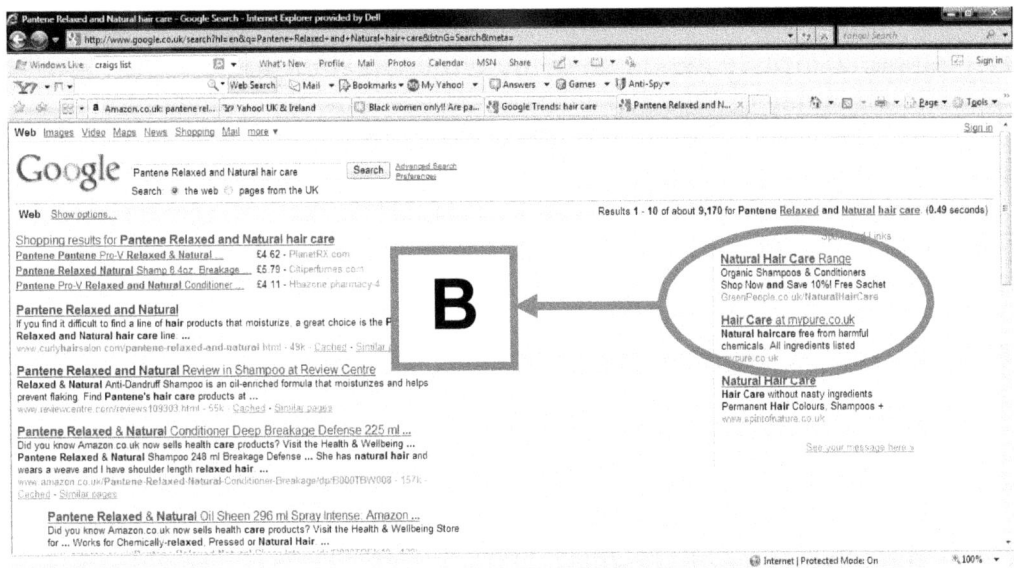

- However, when I made subtle changes to the search terms by using "Pantene Relaxed and Natural range" – **there were no adverts! This is an opportunity to promote products from Amazon.**

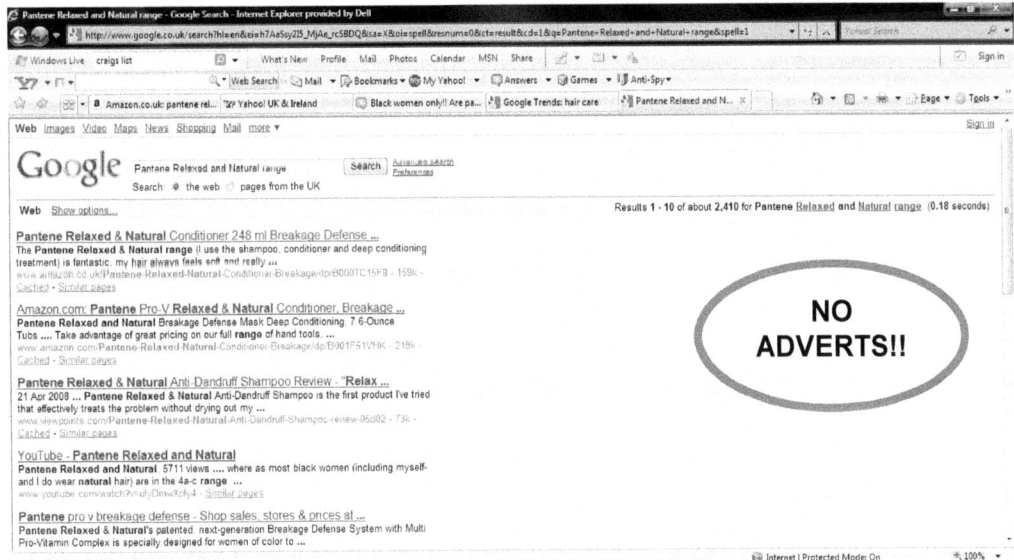

STEP 2 – Creating another free website or webpage

In reference to chapter 4, first of all set up a new website or page.

Remember to include the name of the product(s) that you want to promote on behalf of Amazon. To support the new opportunity I found on Google in the previous step, the name of this next website is www.relaxedandnatural.yolasite.com

This website address can now be used when opening a new affiliation account with Amazon.

STEP 3 - How to register your affiliation with Amazon

- First of all, please go to www.amazon.co.uk . Scroll right down to the bottom of page and click on the "Associates Programme" link marked as C below. (Some screens may vary when companies refresh their page designs).

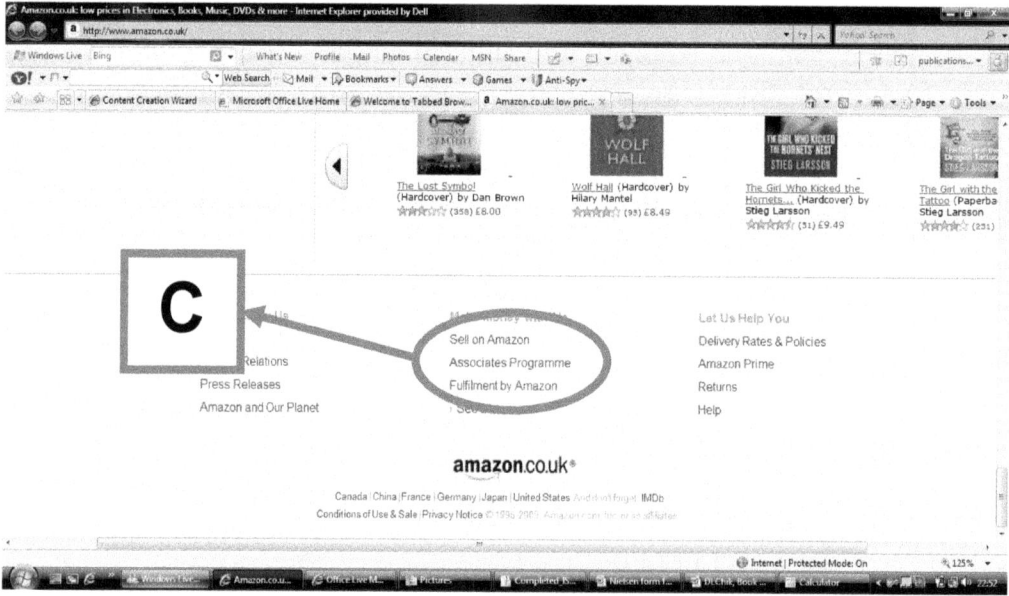

- The page below will appear. Click on the "Join now for free" button marked as D.

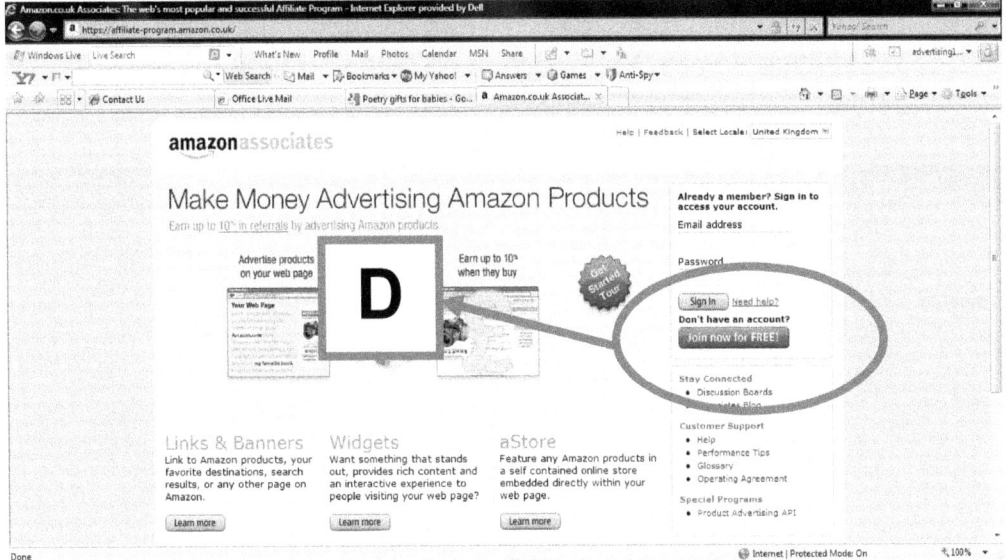

- Next, the page below will appear. Even if you have an existing account that you have used to purchase personal gifts for yourself or others, select the option "I am a new customer" so that you can keep your online income activities separate from your personal purchasing. Enter your dedicated email address into the field marked as E below:

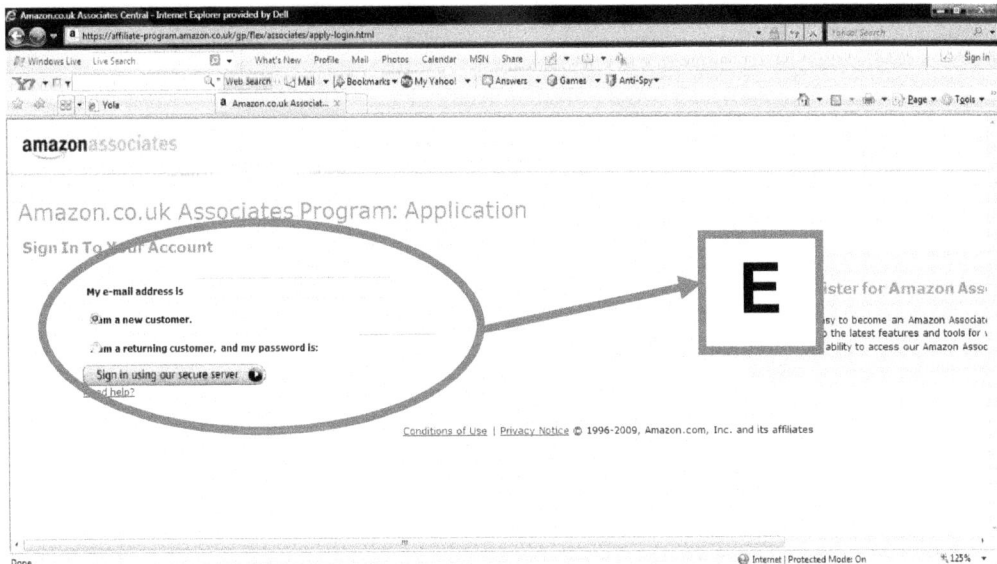

- The next page that appears will ask you to complete your registration details. You will then be taken through to the page below.

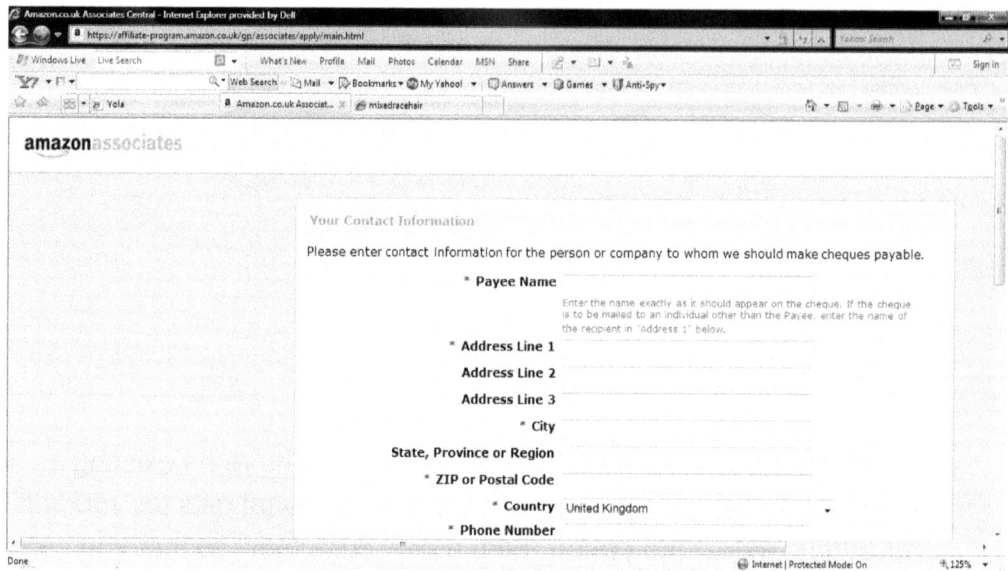

- Once you complete the details, the page below will appear confirming that details have been accepted.

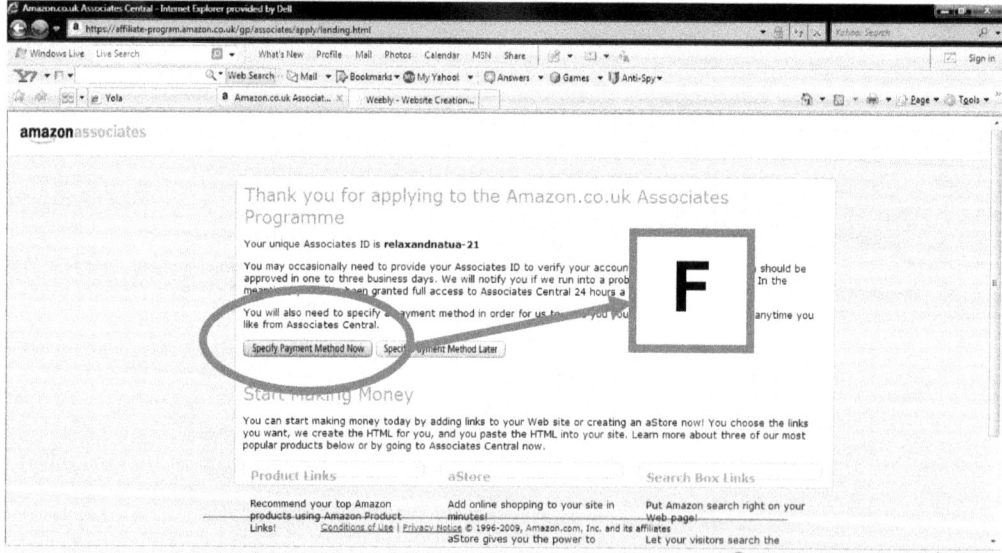

- You will be asked to confirm your payments methods. Click on the "Specify payment method now" button marked as F.

- You can choose to have payments paid directly into your dedicated account. Complete the details and save. The options that appear on the page have been marked for you on the next page.

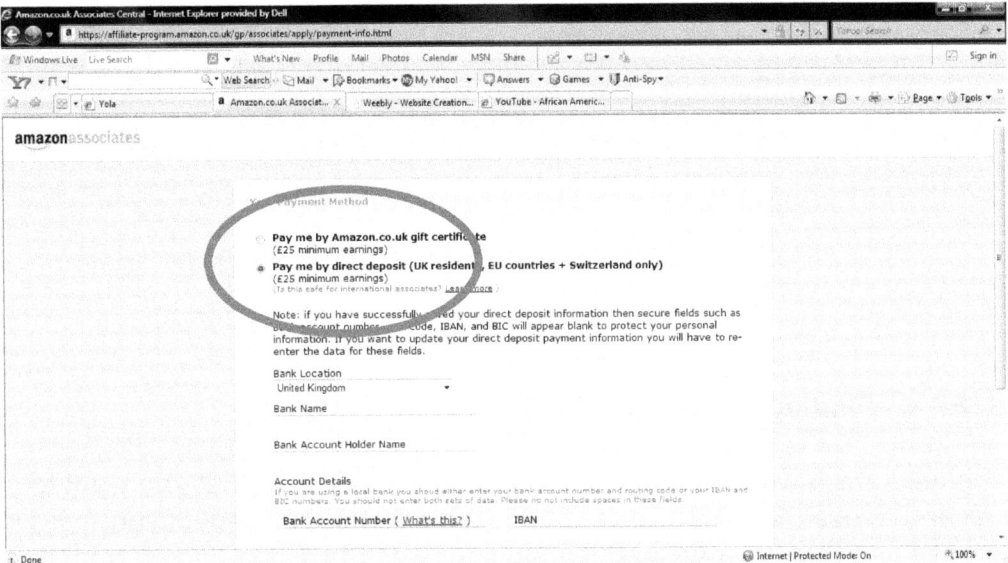

- You will be given an identity number so that Amazon will be able to confirm your affiliation with them marked as G below. THIS IDENTITY NUMBER IS IMPORTANT.

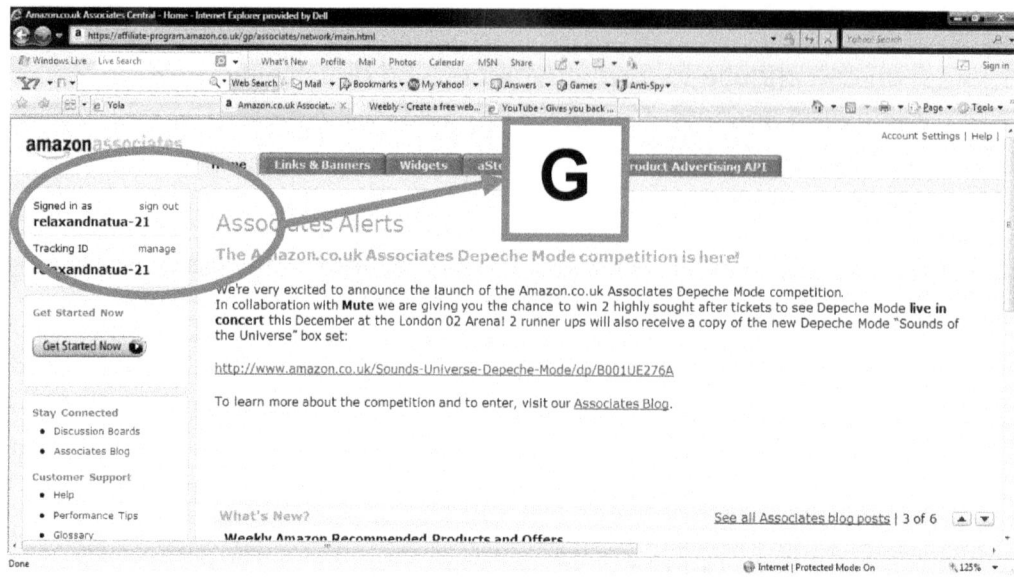

STEP 4 - Finding the product(s) you want to promote

The next steps will show you how to find the product(s) that you want to sell and to use the HTML code (that is specific for the product you choose), so that you can load this on your website. Following on from the steps completed in the previous step:

- At the top of the page click on the "Links and Banners" tab marked as H.
- Next click on the "Add Product Links now" marked as I.

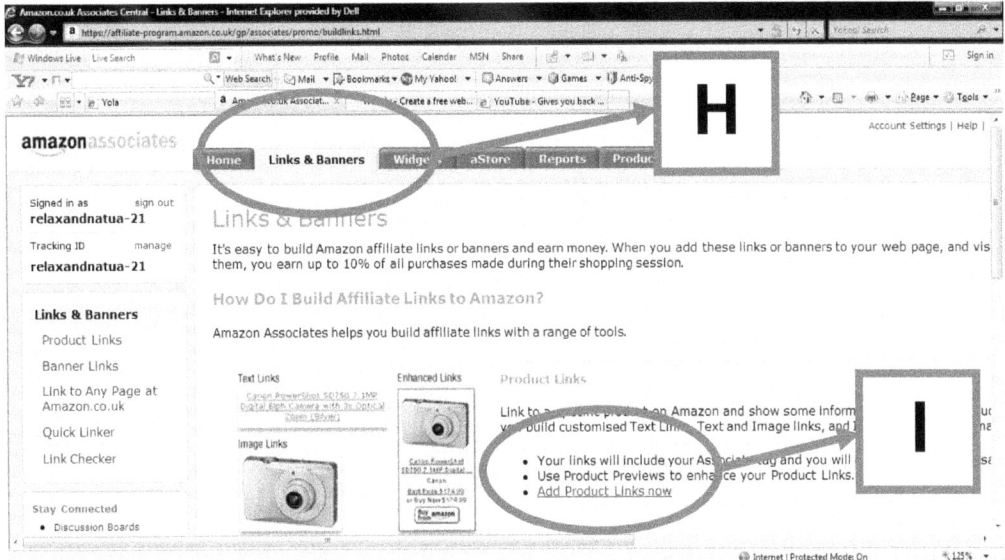

- The page below will appear. Enter the name of the product you want to promote. For this example, I searched for "Pantene Relaxed & Natural Conditioner 645ml." This is marked as J below.

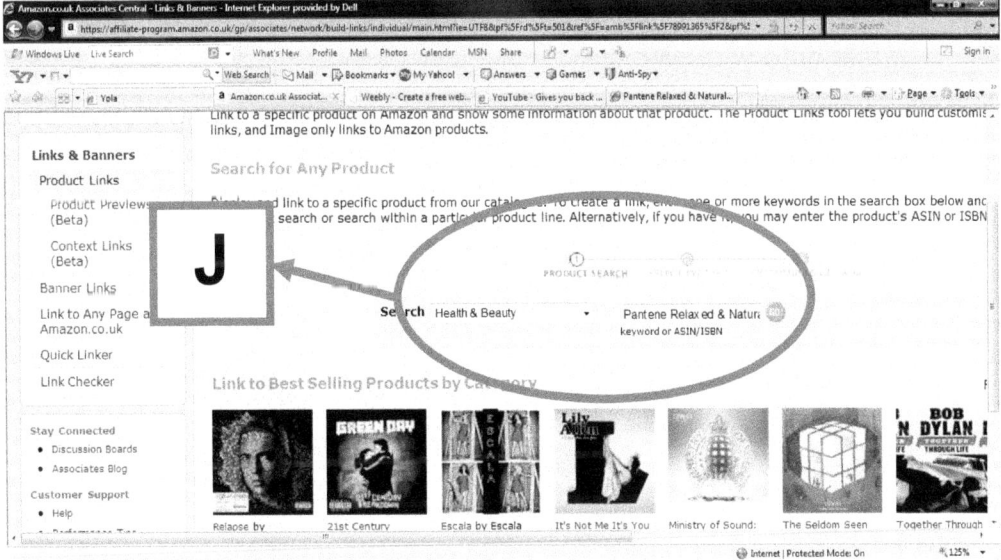

- The next page that appears will show a list of products that match or which relate to your chosen product. Decide on the product you want to promote and then click on the relevant "Get Link" button marked as K.

99

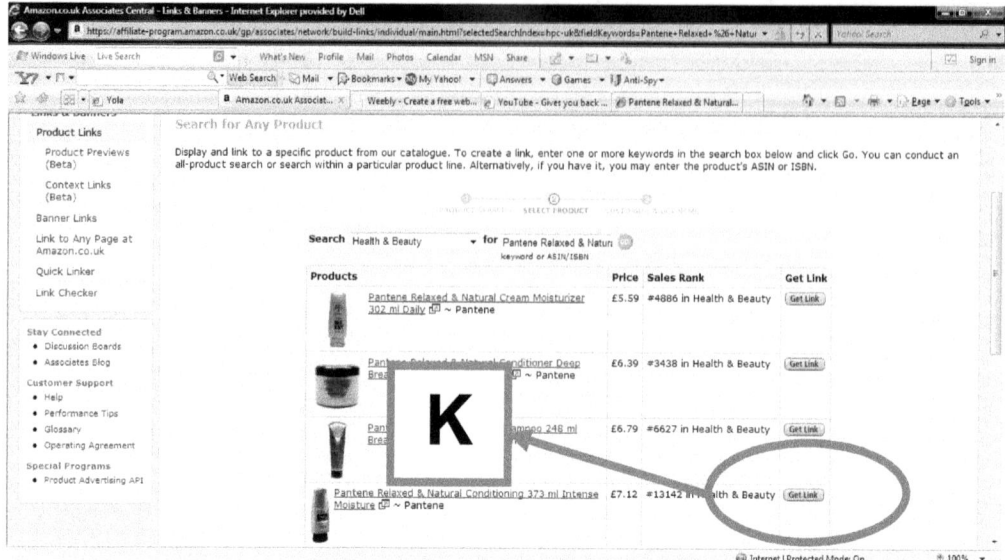

- The next page that appears will show the product that you selected (marked as L) and the HTML code (marked as M) that needs to be added to the website that you created earlier on in this chapter. Copy the HTML code by clicking the "Highlight HTML" button and paste onto your website.

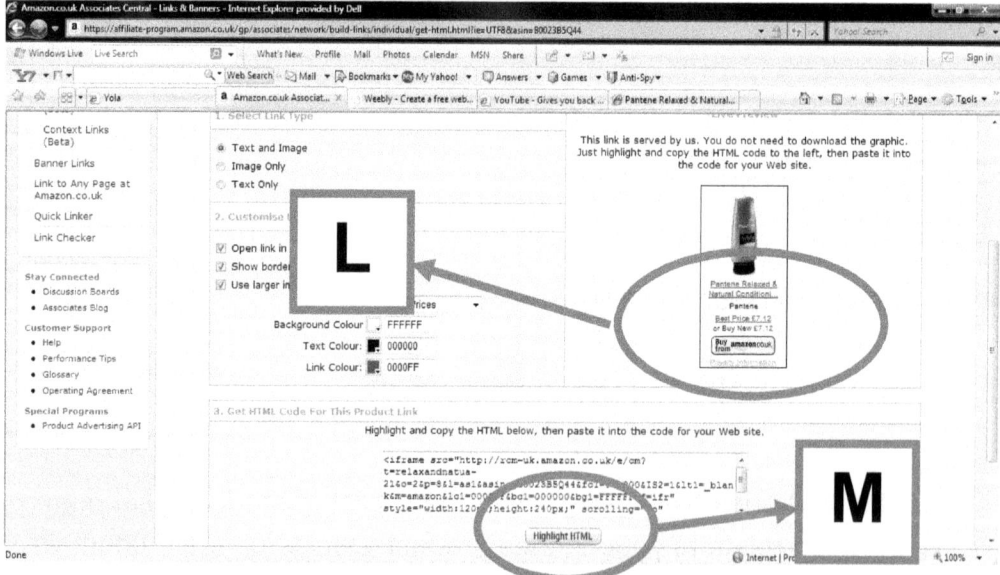

- Once you paste the HTML on your website, ensure that you save any changes. You can view my example at: www.relaxedandnatural.yolasite.com.

TIP – You can add content to review the product(s) on your website. If you do not have any first-hand knowledge of your product, do a quick Google or Yahoo search to see if other searchers have given their opinions of a product or service. You will often find honest reviews from forum sites such as "Yahoo Answers" for example.

Creating a direct advertising link to products on Amazon

In an ideal world, it would be great if every link we search directed us straight to a relevant service or product. This method does just that!

Creating a direct advertising link is different from finding a product on Amazon you want to load onto your website for potential searchers or customers to buy. With this method, you will create a Google advert that will take someone who clicks on the link straight to the product on Amazon.

- First of all, find the product that you want to promote on Amazon. For this example, promoting the music album by Eminem (the Relapse album) will be used.

- Go to www.amazon.co.uk , scroll down and click on the "Associates Programme" link at the bottom of the page marked as N below.

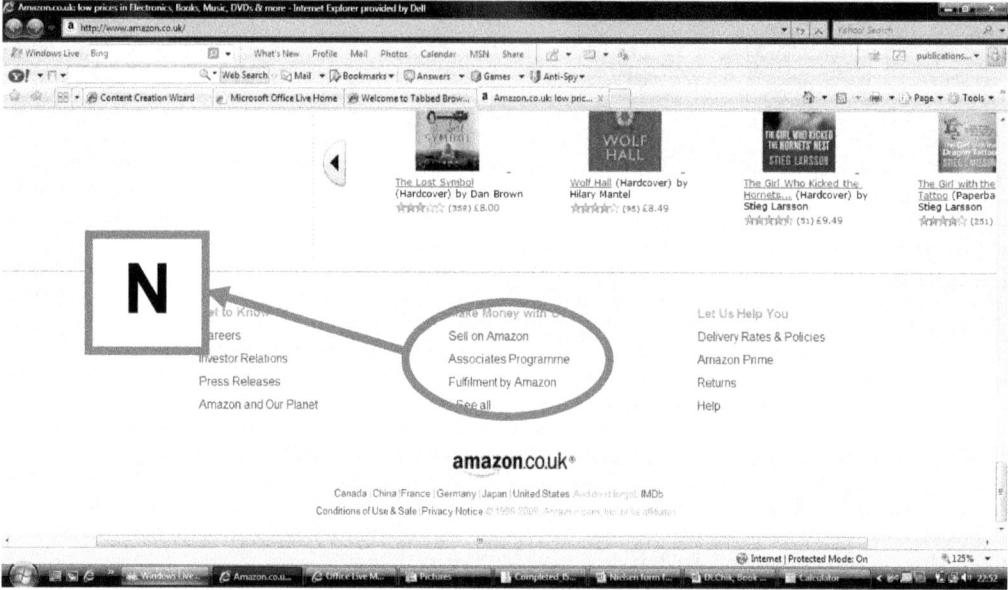

- You will be taken to the home page for Amazon Associates which you will recognise because this is where you had to go to join Amazon's affiliation programme.

- Using your dedicated email address and password log into the website marked as O below and then click on the "Sign in" button.

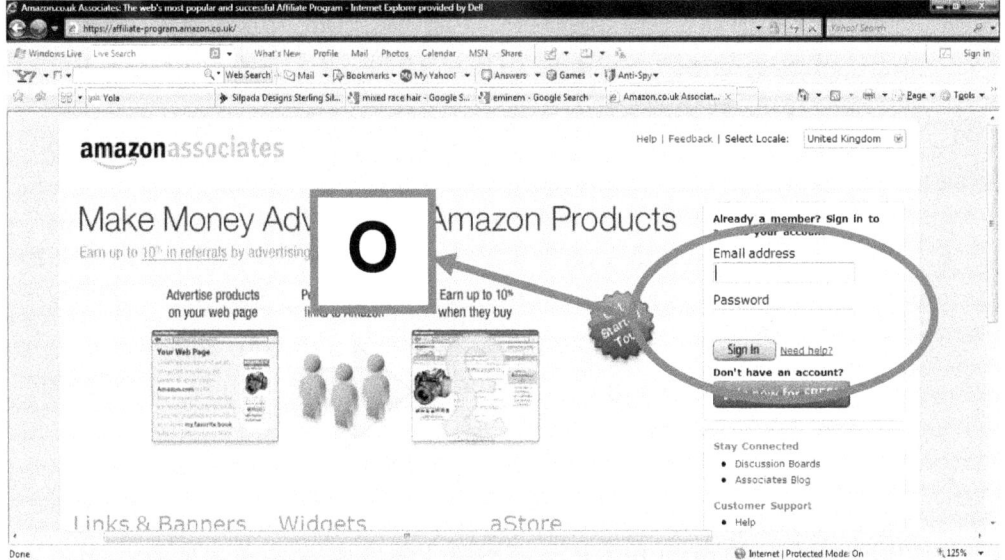

- The page below should look familiar to you. You will need your tracking ID number that Amazon has allocated to you for this promotion method. THIS IS IMPORTANT. To remind you, your tracking ID number will be located in the place marked P below.

***IMPORTANT:** Remember to note your own ID number, not this one in the example!

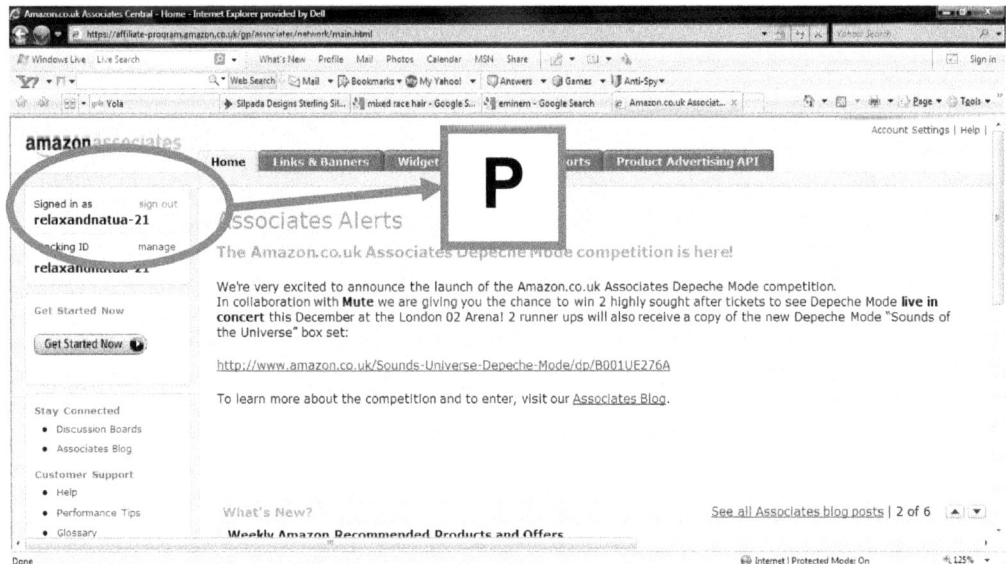

- You can sign out of this screen (the "sign out" link is also marked as P above) once you have **ACCURATELY** noted your ID number.

TIP – Highlight and copy your ID number and paste it onto a blank page in Word so that you can copy and paste it again later on.

- Next you will have to locate the product that you want. Go back to www.amazon.co.uk and search for the product that you want to promote. For this example, I searched for Eminem's Relapse album. Enter the product you want to promote in the search field marked as Q below and press "Go."

TIP – Remember before you decide on the product that you want, you can conduct your own Google (and keyword) searches to see how many adverts exist or how many times the keywords you want to use are used.

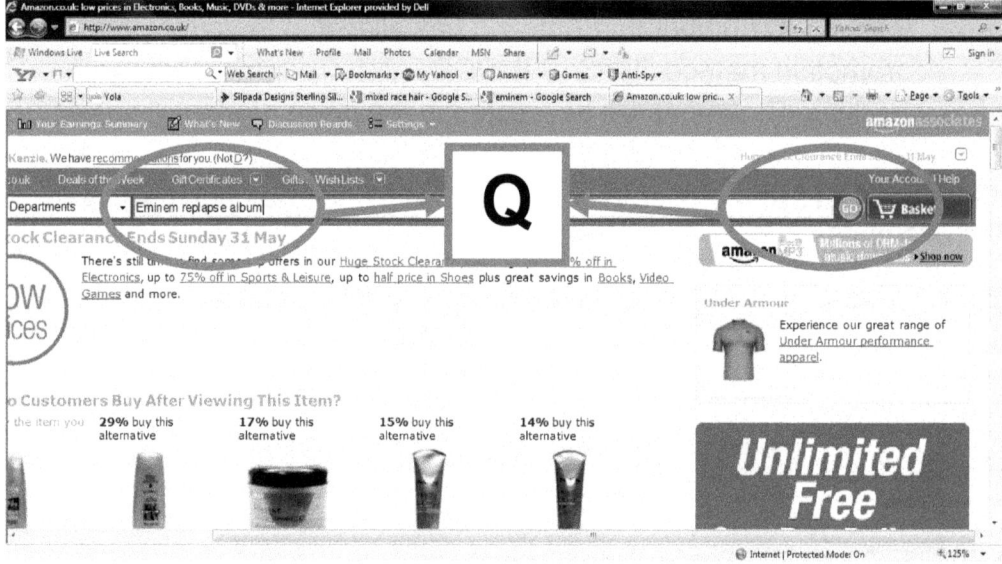

- After you have searched for the product you want and you are happy with your choice, click on the product for more information marked as R below.

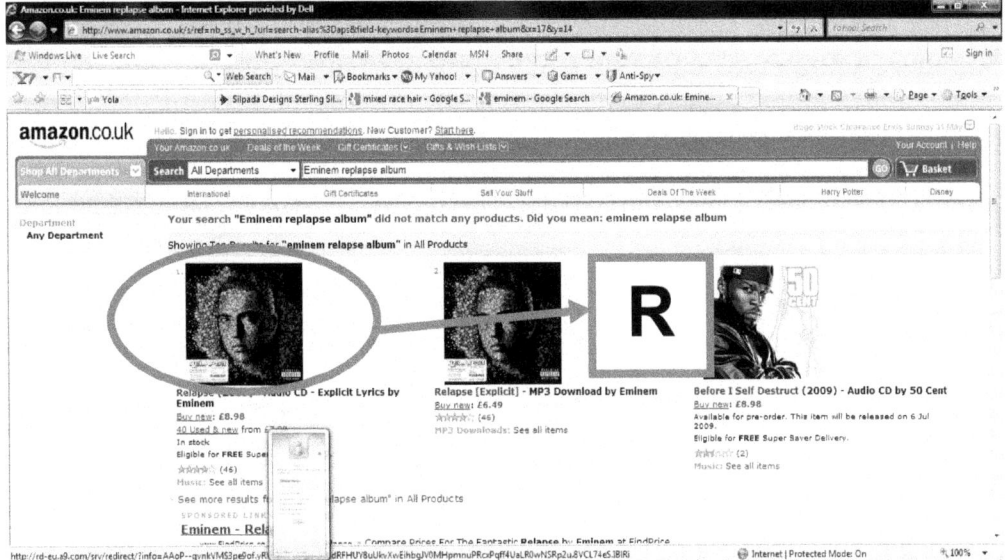

- Next a page will appear where your product choice and some further details are displayed such as a customer review(s), the price of the product etc.

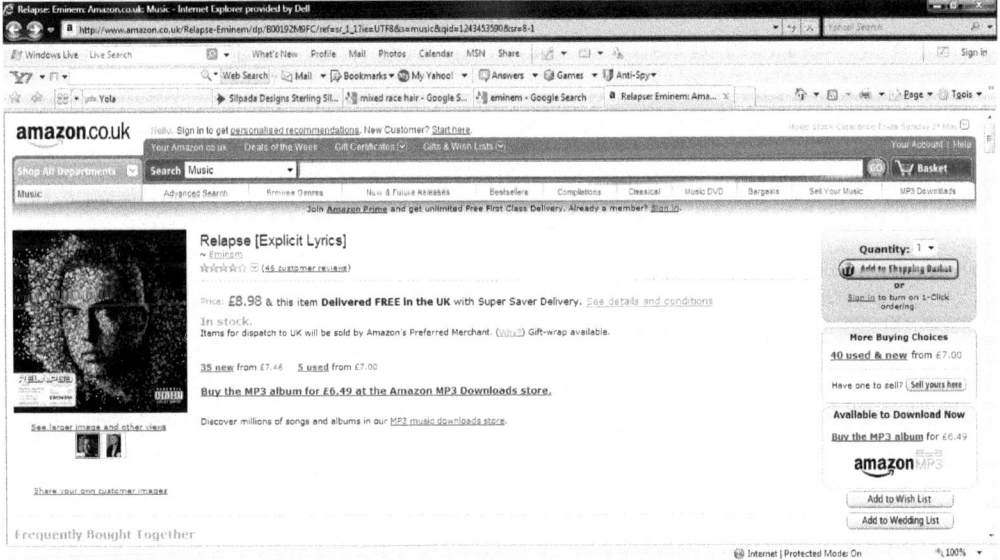

- Scroll down to the bottom of the page. To the left of the page you will see the "ASIN" number for the product. **TAKE NOTE OF THIS NUMBER marked S.**

NOTE: The "ASIN" number stands for **A**mazon **S**tandard **I**dentification **N**umber. Amazon allocates an ASIN number to every product and is used as a code to identify each item. If the ASIN number of a product is known, this can be used to search directly for an item.

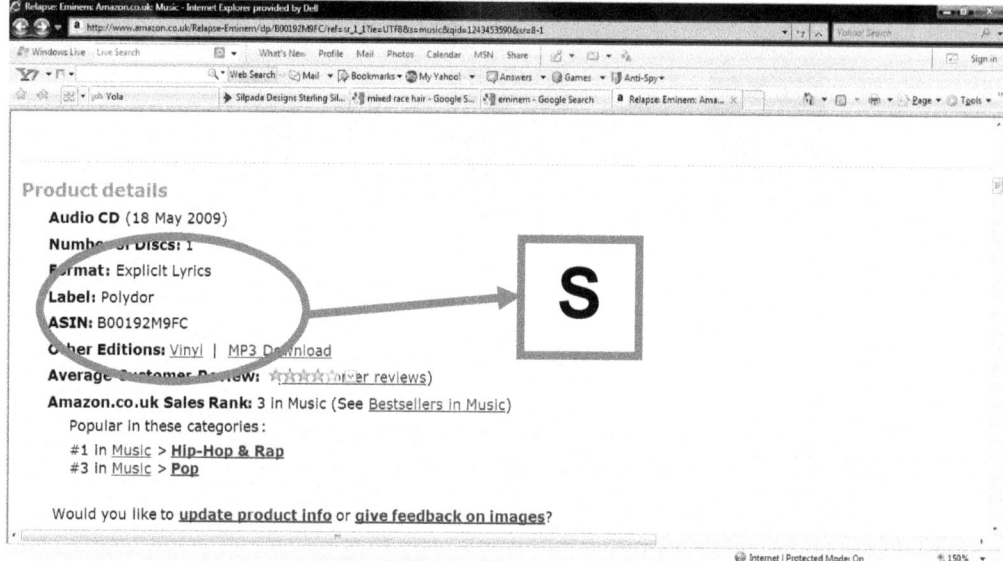

- You will need to use the following code when you create another Google Adwords advert:

www.amazon.co.uk/exec/obidos/ASIN/**asin number**/ref=nosim/**associate ID** number

- For each link that you create for each product that you choose to promote, you will replace "asin number" in the link above with the actual ASIN number for the product; "associate ID" in the link above will be replaced with your personal ID number that Amazon allocated to you, which you took a note of earlier.

For my example of promoting Eminem's Relapse album" the link would appear like this:

- www.amazon.co.uk/exec/obidos/ASIN/B00192M9FC/ref=nosim/relaxandnatua-21

- The next step will be to log into your Google Adwords account to create a new advert. In the field marked as T below, the destination URL will be the link you create for your product.

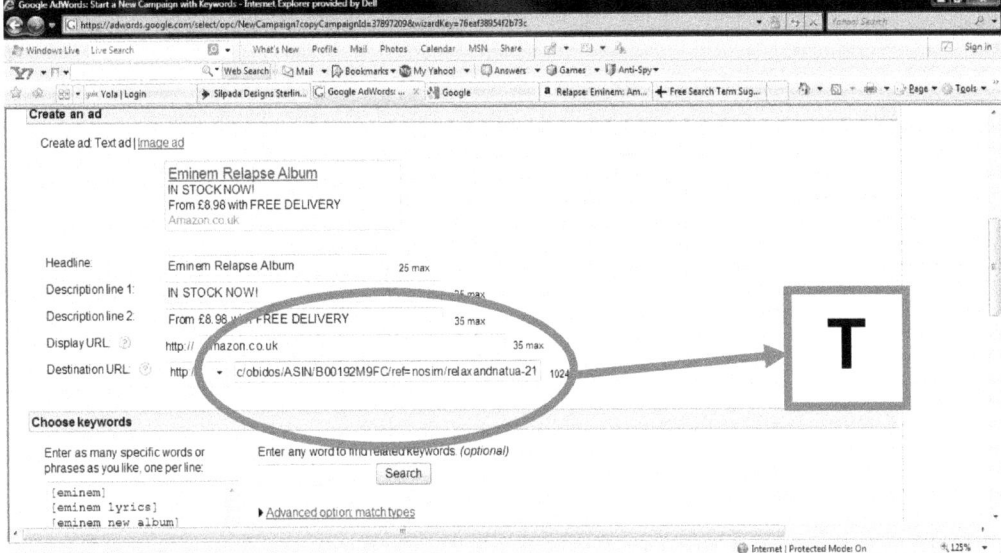

- Once you are happy with the wording of your text, save your campaign.

- My example advert for Eminem's Relapse Album is below - marked as U.

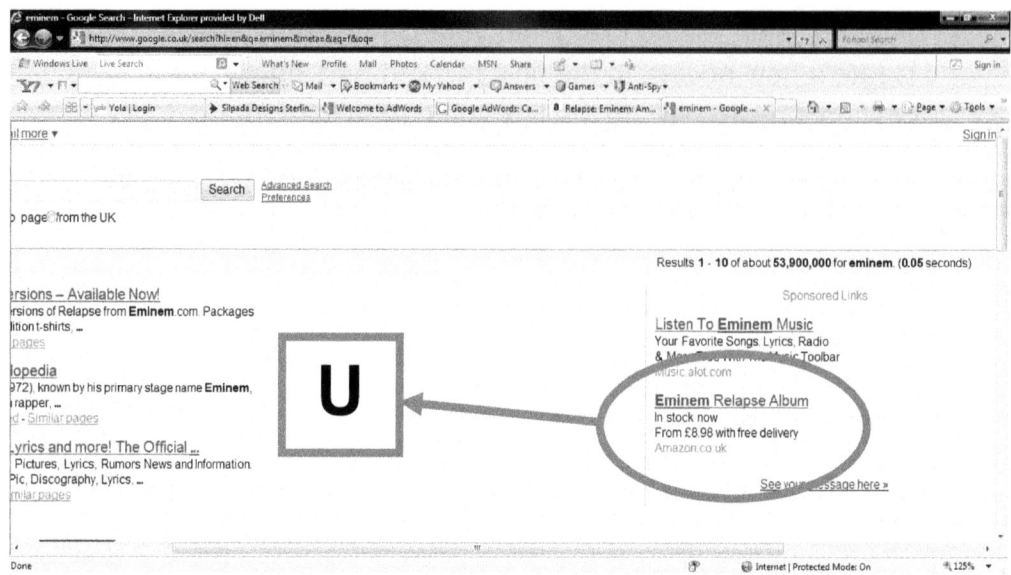

Chapter 8 - Using APPs to generate the income you want

To re-cap from the previous chapter, so far you have:

- Identified a product(s) on Amazon to promote including how to use Google Trends to gain an overview of possible areas to explore.

- Conducted a Google search to identify opportunities for placing an online advert

- Registered an affiliation account with Amazon and learnt how to link products directly to a website you have created to specifically promote a product(s).

- How to set up a direct link from your Google advert to a product that you want to promote on behalf of Amazon.

Apart from companies such as Amazon, there are a number of affiliate programmes that you can join for FREE! The most popular Affiliate Programme Providers (APPs) include:

- Share A Sale
- Azoole Ads
- Clickbank
- Commission Junction (CJ)
- Linkshare
- Trade Doubler
- PayDotCom
- Webgains.com

For this example, we will look at how you can use Clickbank.

What is Clickbank?

Clickbank is the largest online affiliate marketing network. It allows businesses/ merchants to create accounts so that they can load their products and/ or services on Clickbank's website. Affiliates (i.e. people like you and I) can join their affiliate programme to select products to promote and in return receive commission each time that a sale is made.

There is a spectrum of products to choose from, in fact there are thousands. The first step as always is to join the affiliate programme.

TIP – There are thousands of products to choose from, but remember the rule "Think narrow and deep." Refer back to the customer profile that you created earlier (from chapter 3). This will prevent you from wasting time and will help you to focus on relevant products.

- Please go to www.clickbank.com. The following page should appear. Under the Affiliates title, click on the "Sign-up" link marked as A below.

TIP – If you want to learn more about the Clickbank process and how it works you can click on the green "Learn More" button on the home page.

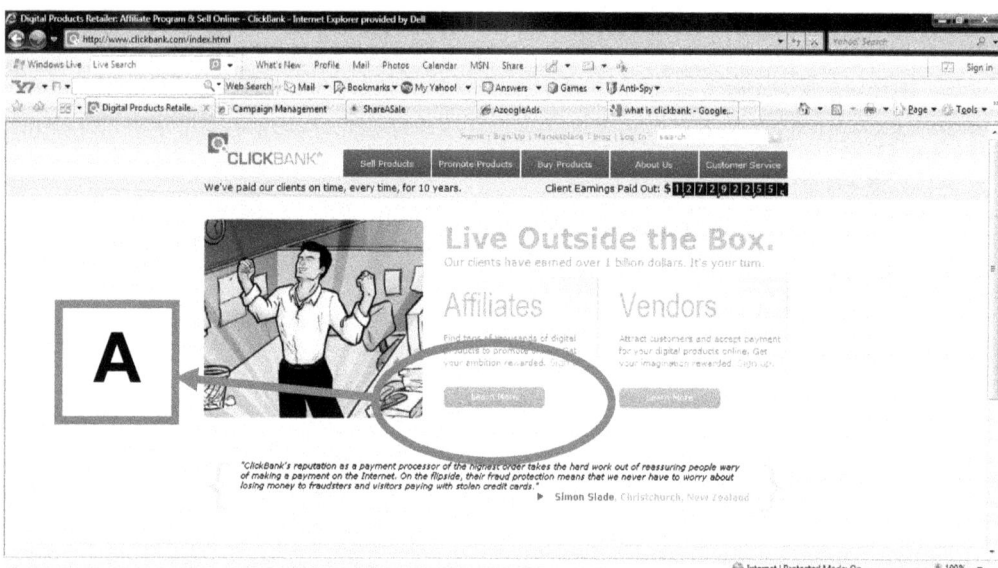

- The page below will appear. Complete the registration form. Once completed, read the terms and conditions, select the tick box to agree to Clickbank's terms and then click the "Submit" button.

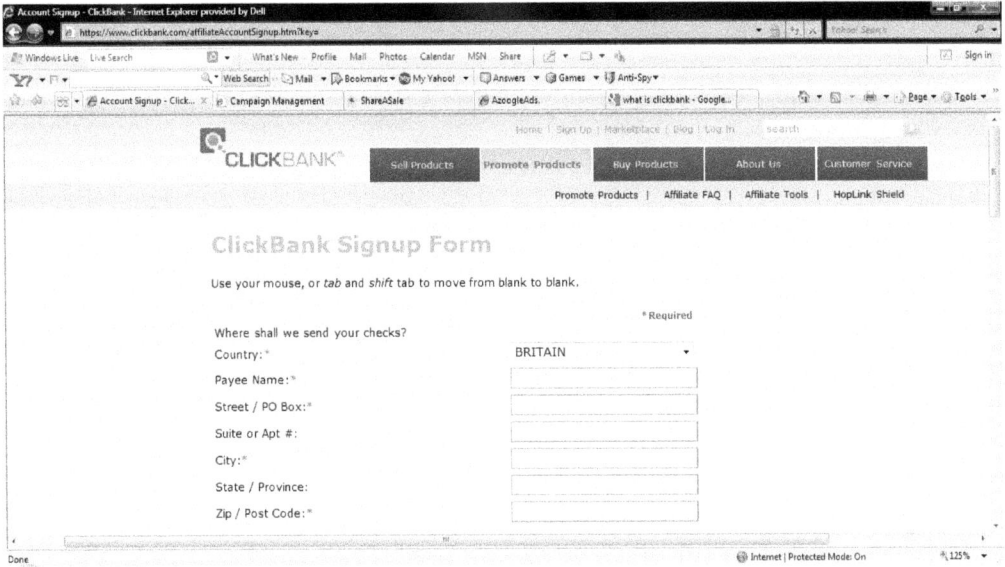

- Once you have completed the form you will be sent an email to approve your account. Once you click the link in your email, you will be taken to a "Congratulations" page, which will confirm your account's username and password.

- Next, the page below will appear. Log into your account by entering your username and password (in the fields marked as B) then click the "Login" button.

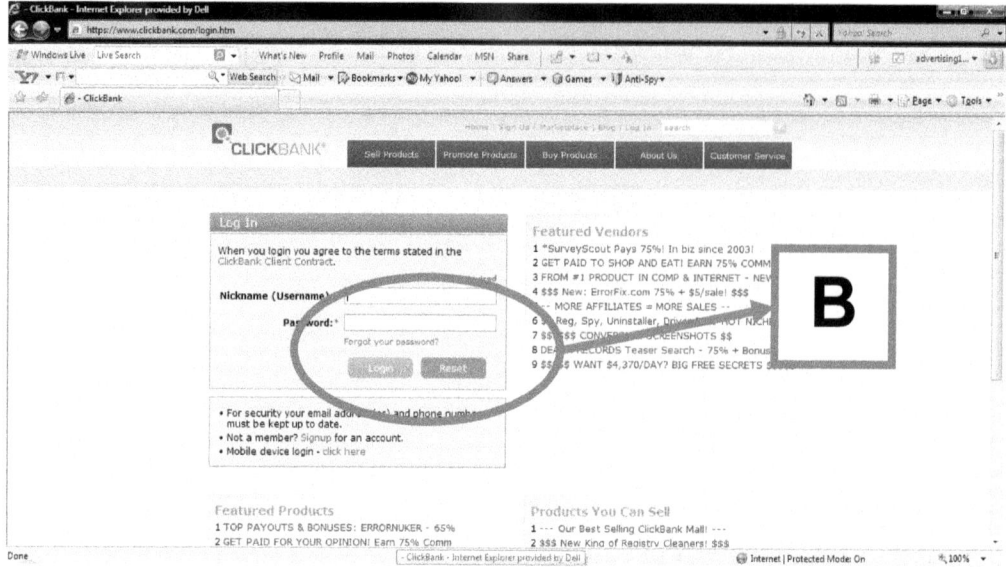

- Once you are logged into your account, the next page will appear. Click on the "Marketplace" link marked as C.

TIP - Going forward, as you promote more products and/ or services you will be able to check your activity and commission sales.

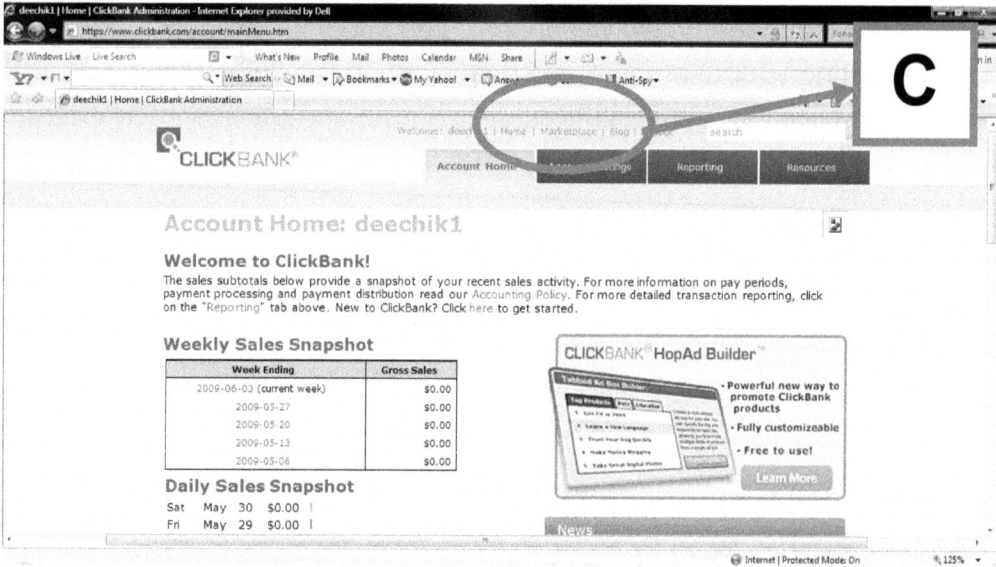

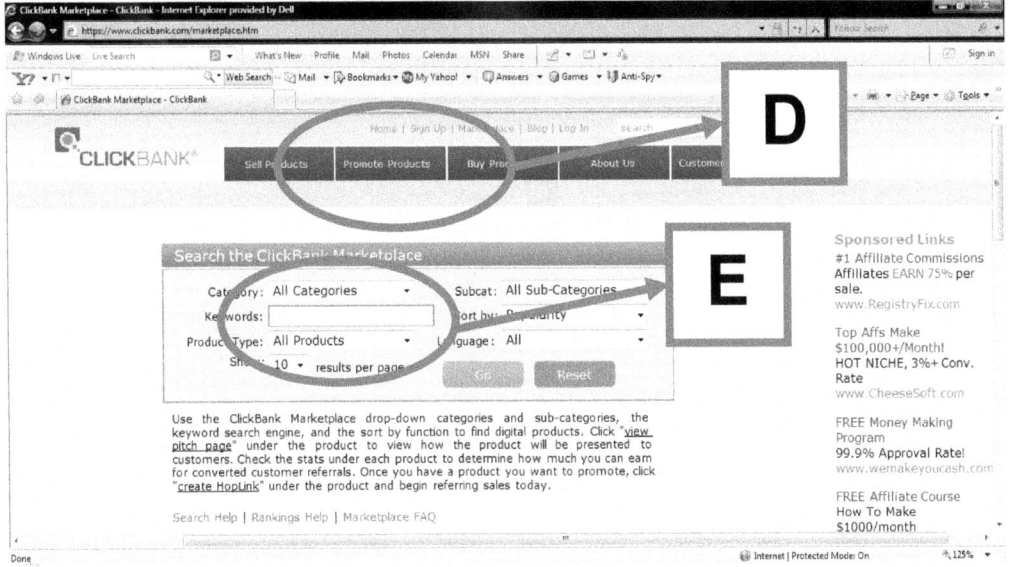

- The page above will appear. Click on the "Promote Products" tab (marked as D) and a search box will appear where you can search for products to promote.

- For this example, we'll choose "Health & Fitness" from the drop down "All categories" menu marked as E. Then click on the "Go" button.

- A page similar to the one below will appear. For this example, we will review the details of product number 5 "Cheat your way thin" marked as F below.

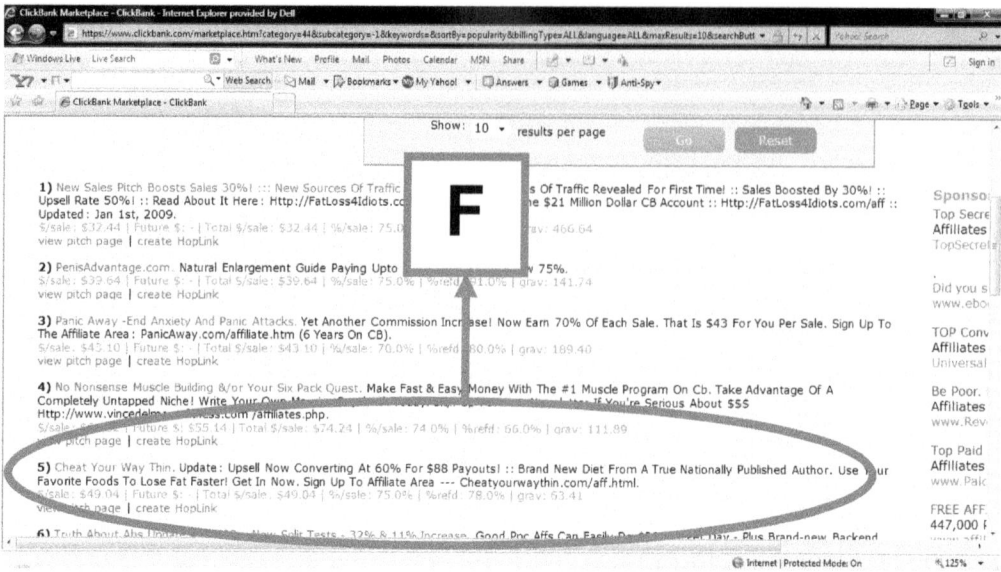

- There are a range of figures that appear as a part of each product's summary. Let's review what the figures in the summary mean:

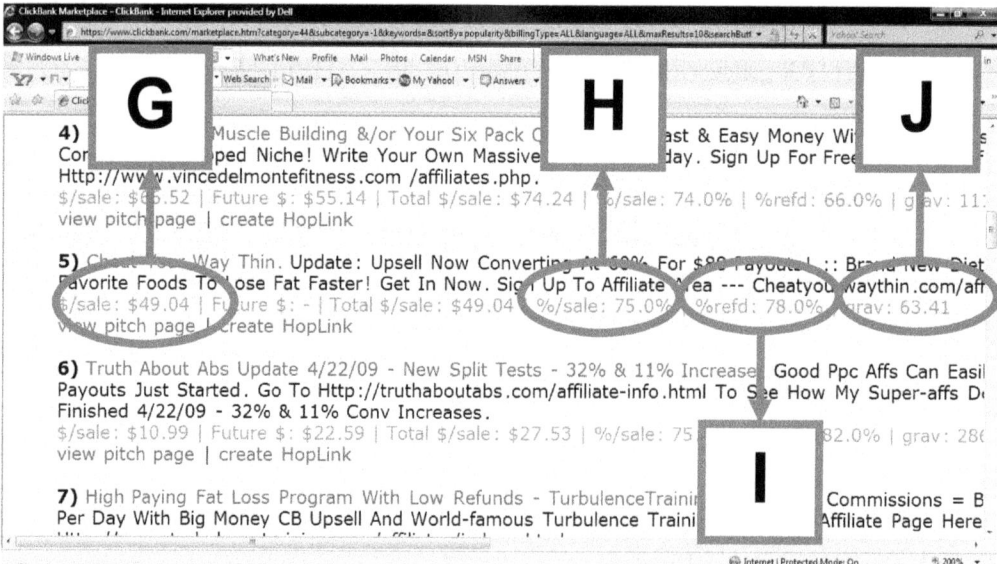

- **Section marked as G** – with each sale that is made as a result of you marketing this product (via creating your adverts using

Google's Adwords), you will receive $49.04 after Clickbank have deducted all their charges.

- **Section marked as H** – This shows that you will make a commission of 75% of the sale price for every product sold.

- **Section marked as I** – This shows the percentage of sales that come from affiliates.

- **Section marked as J** – This shows the number of affiliates that are currently selling this product i.e. the *Gravity*.

TIP 1 – By sticking to your theme or niche customer profile that you created back in chapter 3, do your best to identify/ short-list 5-10 products to promote initially.

TIP 2 – Identify products that have a *gravity* (i.e. the number of affiliates currently promoting the product) between 10 – 100. Any products that have below 10 affiliates promoting the product suggests that the product is yet to be proven; any products that have over 100 affiliates promoting it means that this is already being promoted fairly heavily. You can choose to promote any product, since you may find that you can find other opportunities to market a product – for example by using alternative keywords.

TIP 3 – Click on the "View pitch page" link in the product summary to read about the product. Ask yourself if the pitch has enough information to convince you or a potential customer to purchase the product or is it nonsense?

TIP 4 – Use the "sort by" drop down menu to search for products to consider. For example, you can sort by "Low Gravity" to check the number of affiliates that are currently promoting the product. See the section marked as K below:

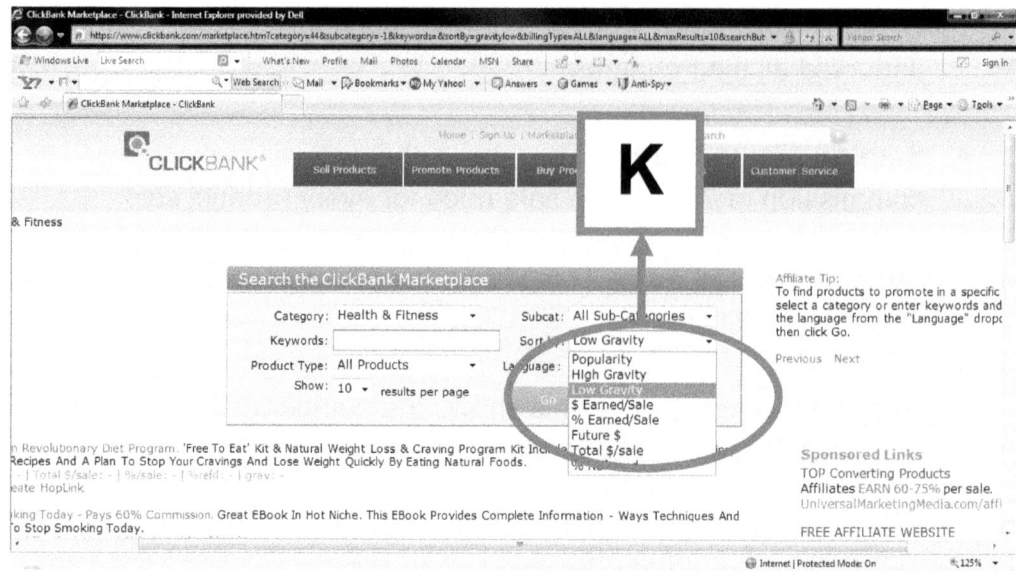

Promoting your chosen Clickbank product(s)

After selecting the products that you want, you can create Google Adword campaigns so that searchers can be directed straight to the links of the website that pitch the products that you have selected.

Alternatively, the product(s) you have chosen to promote can be featured on your own "review" website or blog. The key thing is to write a short article that reviews the product(s) that you are promoting and to include a link to your new website link. The article you write can be loaded on a website that reviews other products. Within the article on your website, you then include the direct hoplink (that you create in ClickBank) that directs searchers to the original pitch or sales letter that you reviewed previously before choosing to promote that product.

Before writing the article, the next step is to set up another free web page or blog. To create a blog, you can visit any of the following sites and open an account:

- www.socialgo.com
- www.wordpress.com
- www.blogger.com
- www.thoughts.com

For this example, I set up an account at www.blogger.com . If you choose to use this provider, click on the "Create your own blog now" arrow marked as L below.

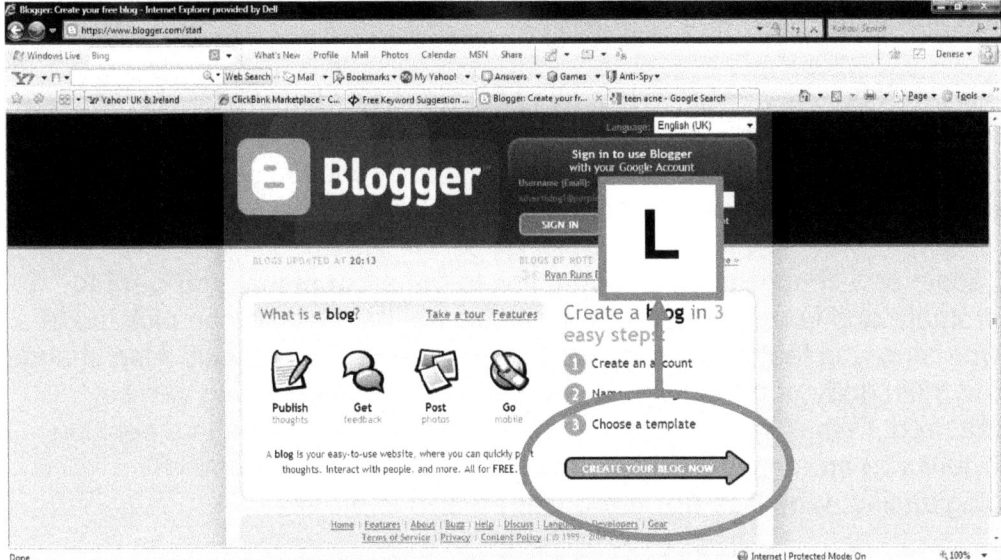

- The page below will appear. Click on the "Sign in first" blue link (marked as M below) and follow the instructions. You can sign in using your username and password for the Google Adwords account that was previously created.

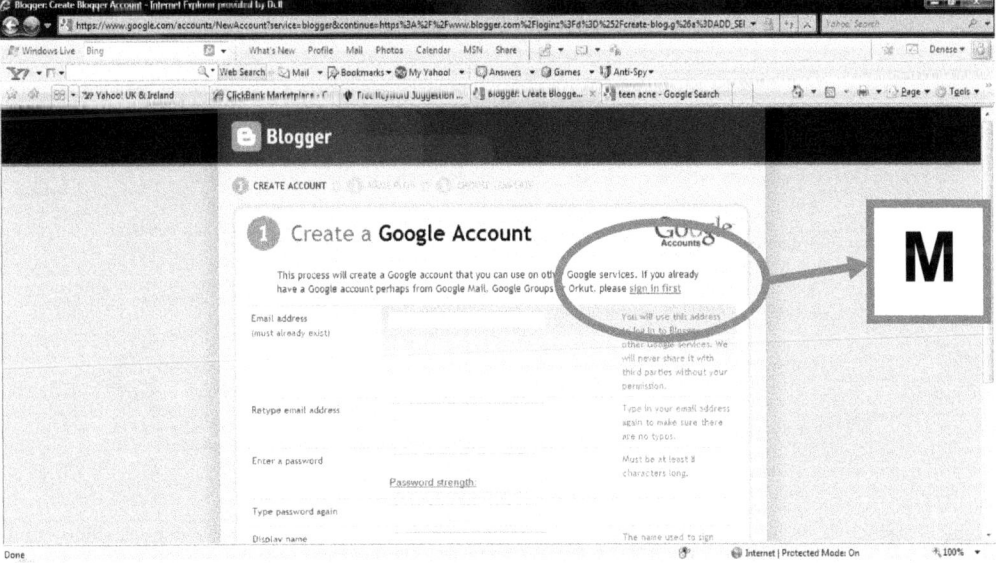

117

Writing your review article

After you have opened a Blog account, you can draft your article about the product(s) you want to promote.

TIP – People review products all of the time. Of course you are welcome to purchase the products yourself and to review them first hand, however to save yourself time search for articles that already exist about the product(s) that you want to promote.

Locate and choose keywords that link to the product that you want to promote and feature these in your article so that Google can pick these words up and feature your article as a relevant search result. Also change the main body of the article so that your own style of writing can be featured. This is important because you do not want to be in a position where you are copying an article word for word – that is called plagiarising, **which is not encouraged and is illegal.**

For this example, I chose to promote the product "Acne free in 3 days" marked as N below, to stick with the overall theme of Health/ Fitness and Beauty. The sales letter or pitch can be found at http://www.acnefreein3days.com/c/index.html?hop=0 .

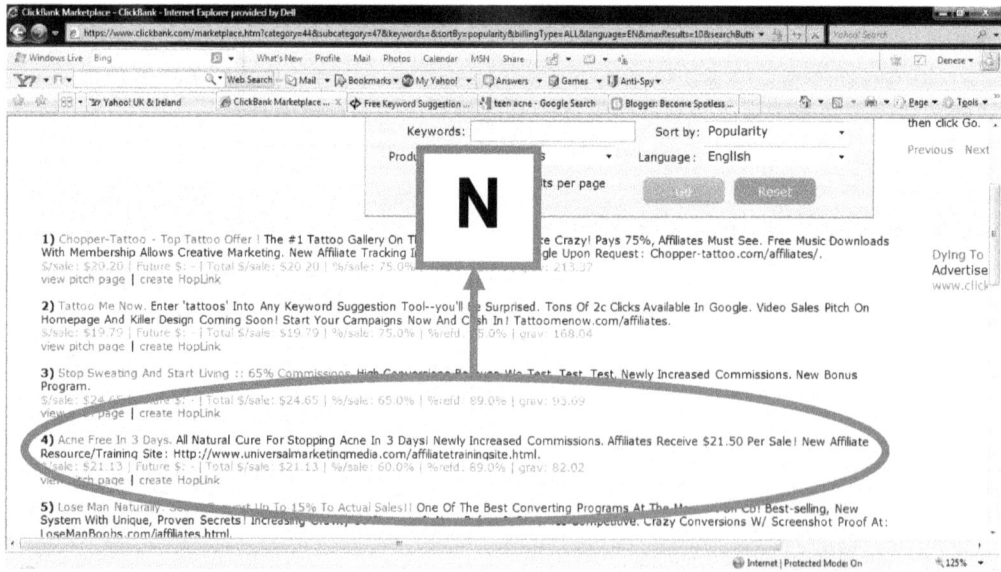

TIP – As mentioned before, you will need to create your "Hoplink" here, but this will be covered shortly.

First locate at least 7 – 10 keywords that relate to your product. You can use the search tool that we used before. For this example of "Acne free in 3 days" I used http://www.keyworddiscovery.com/search.html .

I decided to search for the following phases and/ or words:

- Acne
- Teenage Acne
- Acne treatment
- Spot treatments
- Clear skin
- Acne detox
- Acne free
- Acne free in 3 days
- Spot free skin
- Acne free

After searching for "Acne" first, the following results appeared:

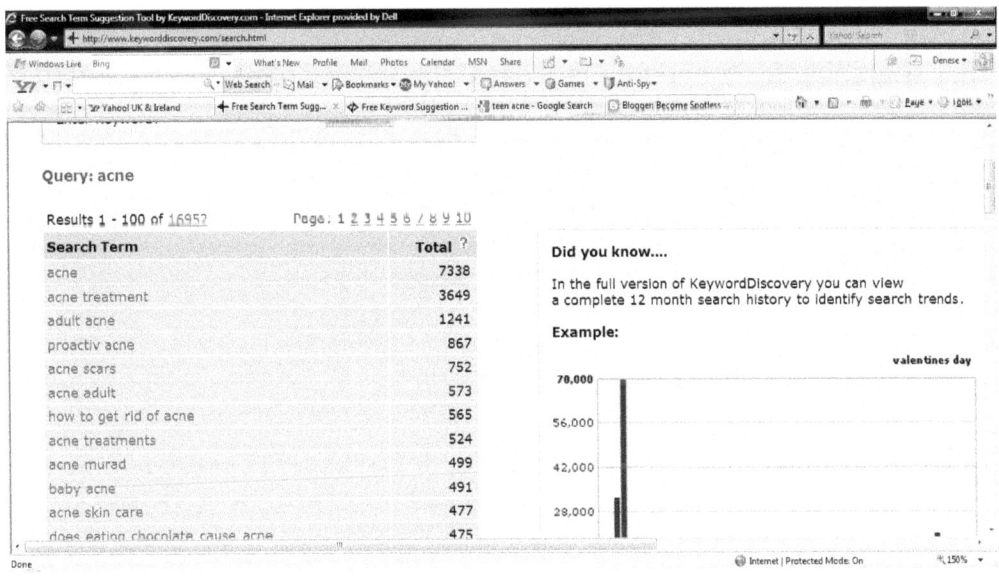

- "Acne" was searched for 7338 times; "Acne treatment" was searched for 3649 times; "Adult Acne" was searched for 1241 times.

After searching for "Clear Skin" the following results appeared:

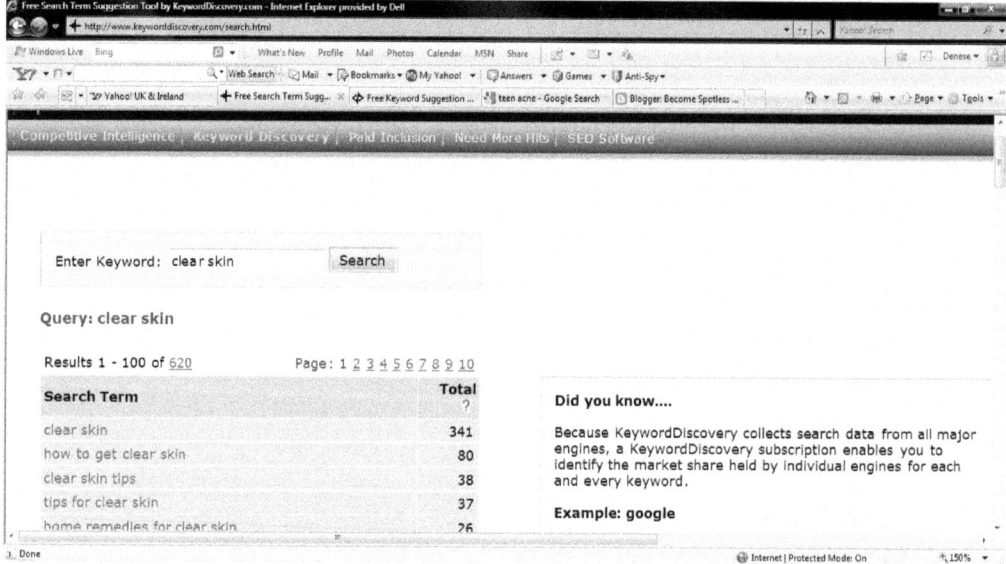

- "Clear skin" was searched for 341 times; "how to get clear skin" was searched for 80 times; "Clear skin tips" were searched for 38 times.

After searching for "Acne free in 3 days" the following results appeared:

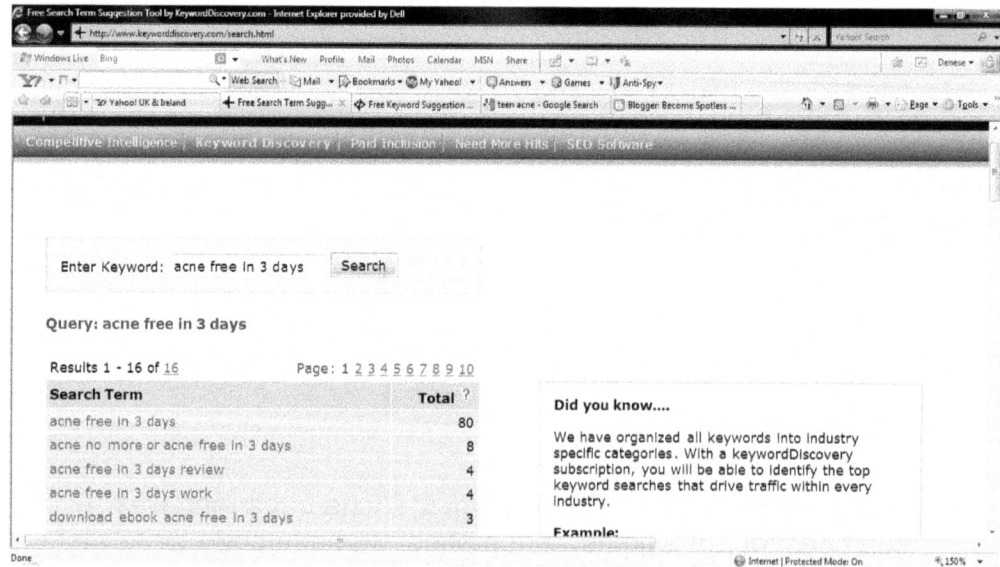

- "Acne free in 3 days" was searched for 80 times; "Acne no more or acne free in 3 days" was searched for 8 times; Acne free in 3 days review was searched for 4 times.

From the results of the above searches, I decided to use the following keywords:

- Acne free in 3 days
- Clear skin
- How to get clear skin
- How to get rid of acne
- Acne
- Acne skin care
- Acne skin treatment

The keywords highlighted above are the main keywords that need to be used most frequently in the article.

TIP 1 – To get the attention of Google, it is best to write your review article with at least 500 – 700 words.

TIP 2 - It is important that you get the density of how often you use your identified keywords balanced so that Google can pick up your site/content for its relevance. If keywords are used excessively, then Google will tend to categorise your website as spam.

You can check the level of density that your keywords have in your article by visiting – http://www.live-keyword-analysis.com. Aim for a density of about 6% for your main keywords that you have to use in your article. If the density is any lower than this Google will assume that your article is not relevant.

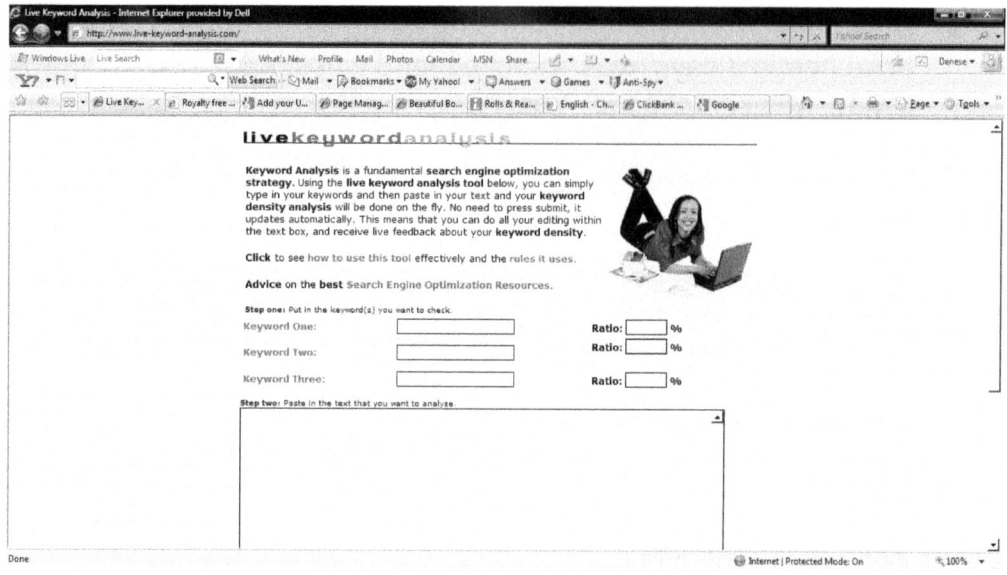

TIP 3 – Ensure that you mention your keywords within the first and last paragraph of your article.

TIP 4 – Include a link to your blog site in your article at least twice to give the reader more than one chance to click on the link to your blog site.

TIP 5 – Create an edited or short version of your original article to submit to the review sites that you use and then feature your full version on your blog. Remember that the version on your blog site MUST feature your Clickbank hoplink, so that readers can click directly to the website that pitches or sells that product(s) or service(s) you are promoting. More of this is covered below.

How to feature your Clickbank hoplink in your article

- First of all log into your Clickbank account and locate the product(s) that you want to promote.

- Then when your product appears click on "Create Hoplink" marked as O:

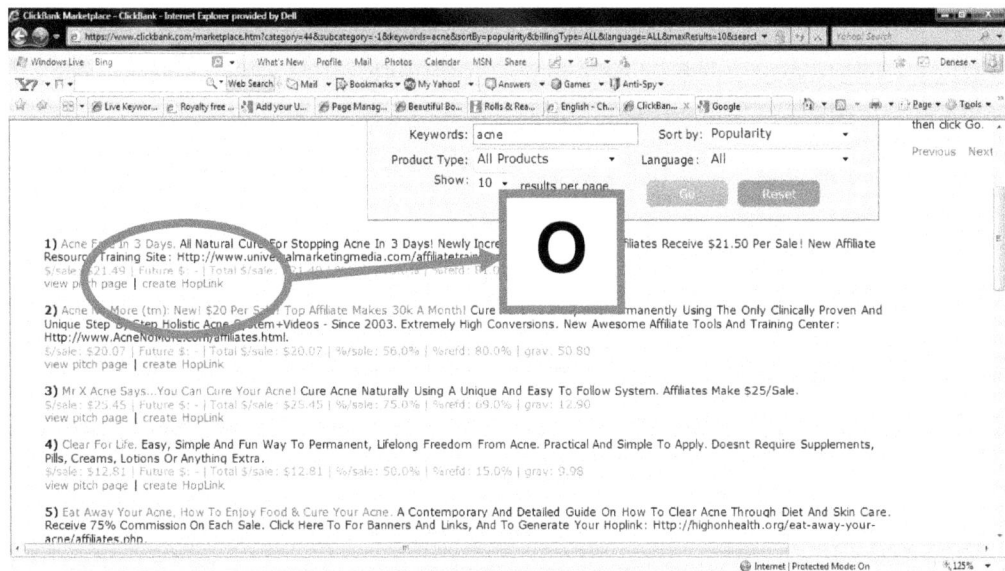

- The following pop-up page will appear. Enter in your Clickbank ID and click on the "create button" marked as P on the next page:

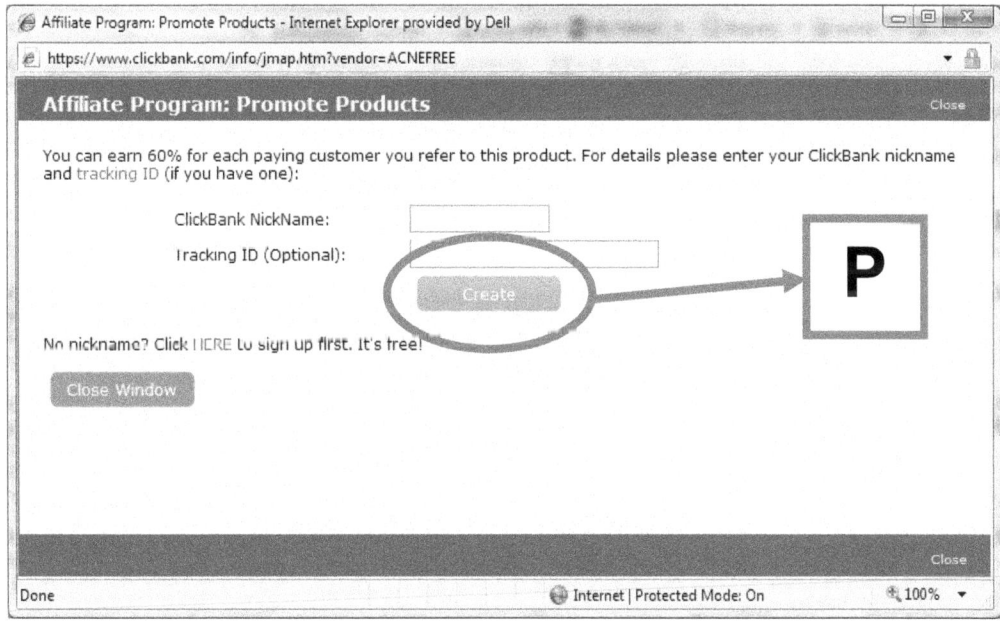

- Another pop-up box will appear which will give you details of the domain name and hoplink that you need to direct customers to. You will need to use the domain name that you have been given.

TIP – Most review sites do not accept domain name links like the one Clickbank advises to give to customers, so instead state the link to your blog address in your article. When searchers click through to your blog site, in the full version of the article you can create URL links to the hoplink address that Clickbank give you.

For example, you can go to my blog site address:

http://becomespotless.blogspot.com . The following page will appear:

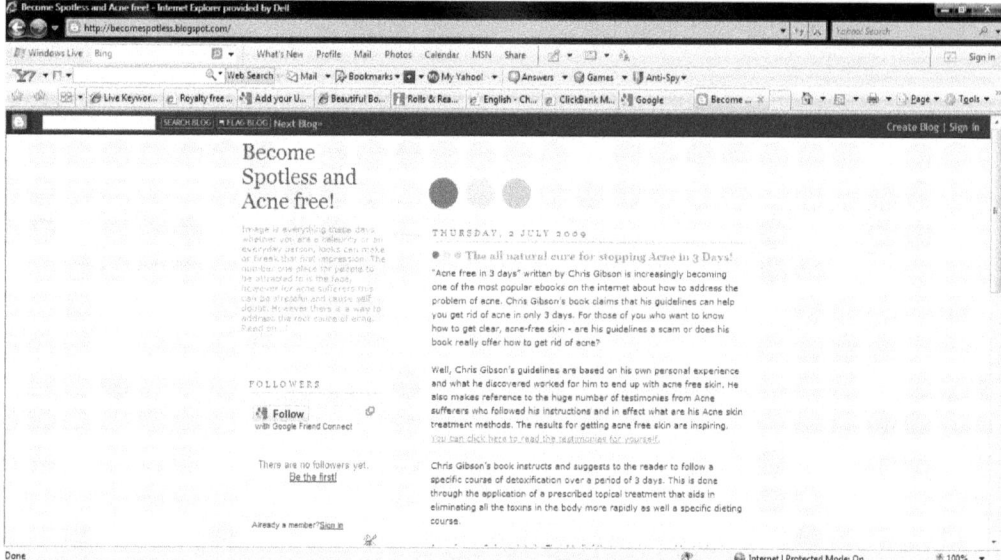

You will notice that I have created two hyperlinks within my article. Each link has been given the URL link of my Clickbank hoplink address to promote the product I have chosen. This means that whenever a searcher clicks on any of these links, they will be taken directly to the sales page for the product(s) that I am promoting.

Once you are happy with your article, you can always test your links to make sure that searchers will be directed to the webpage that you intend for them to see.

Loading your article on review sites

You can load your article at a number of review sites, but as a suggestion you may want to use:

- www.hubpages.com
- www.ezinearticles.com
- www.searchwarp.com
- www.ehow.com

TIP – Be sure to read or take note of any article submission guidelines, since some websites make it very clear that any content that is submitted should not be used for commercial gain or for marketing purposes.

For this example, I will show you how to load your article on www.ehow.com .

- The page below should appear. You will have to register an account to be able to submit an article. Click on the "Write" link marked as Q below:

- The page below will appear. Click on "Register with eHow" marked as R below. You will be directed to a page where you will have to complete your details similar to what you have done before when registering your other accounts.

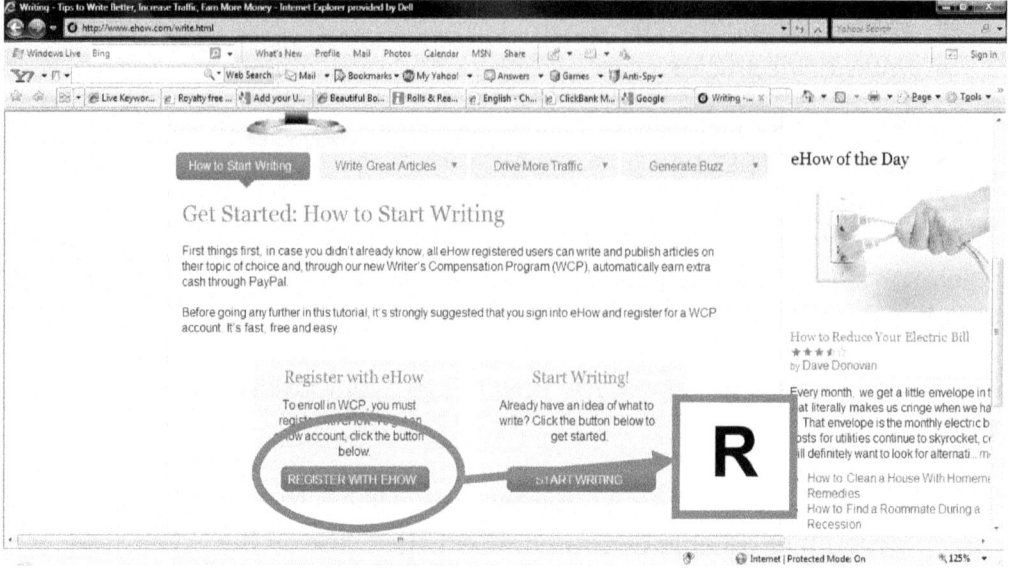

- Once you complete all your details, eHow will send an email to your dedicated email address (i.e. the email address that you stated on your registration form). Take a note of your username and password to sign into this site, i.e. in your dedicated notebook as advised in the beginning of this book.

- Next you can adapt or cut and paste your summarised version of your review article into "how to" steps regarding the subject of your product and then make reference to your blog site address.

- To start writing or adding your article, first of all, type in the title of your article, i.e. my example is called "How to become Acne free" and then click on the "Write" button all marked as S below.

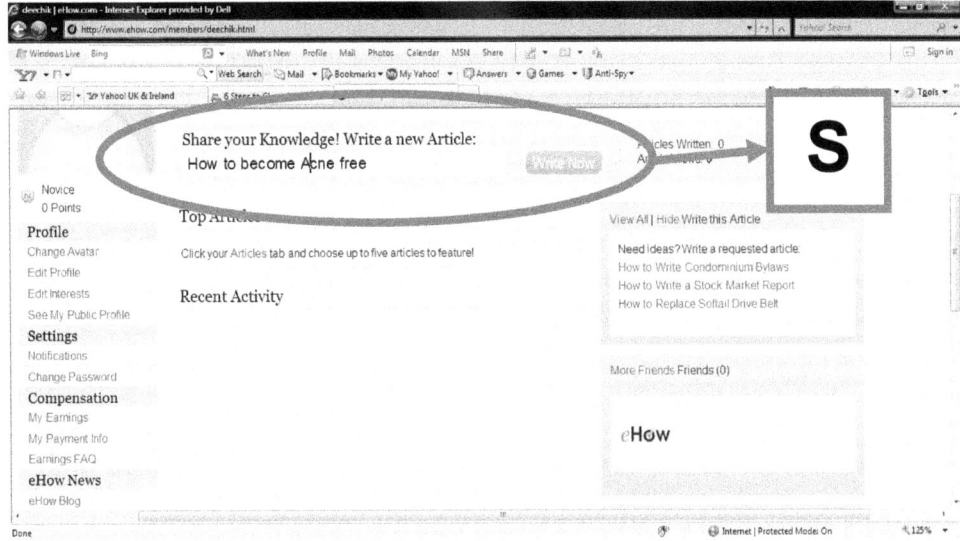

- Next, you will be taken to a page where you can begin to structure your article. There are only three steps to complete before you can publish your article.

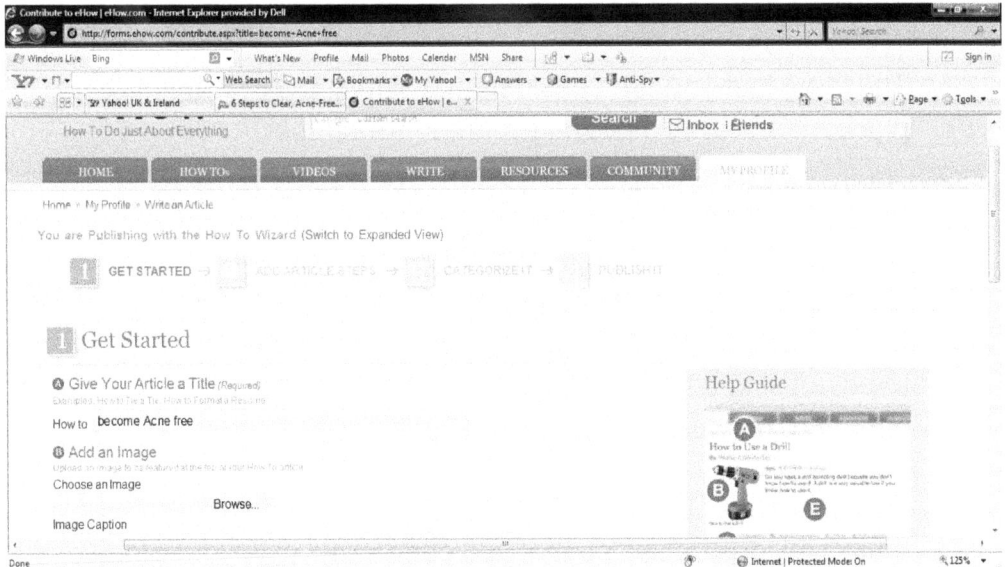

TIP- Remember that you do not have to use just one review website! You can load your article and adapt it to appeal to different audiences. The more exposure you give to your dedicated blog site address(es), then the more opportunities there will be for searchers to refer to your blog site which will connect them to the hoplinks and products you are promoting. Your core aim is to guide as many searchers to the hoplinks of the products you are promoting.

Supporting your articles by advertising with traditional media

Even though the internet has evolved into *the* prominent global network, not everyone has access to the internet on a regular basis and/ or still may not trust using the internet for whatever reason.

Remember the customer profile you created in chapter 3, let's go back!

As a part of your customer profile, you identified the magazines and/ or newspapers that are aimed at your customer profile. Contact these media publications. They often list their contact details within the second or third page of a magazine. Newspapers sometimes place their contact details in the form of an advert in their classifieds section. Once you have identified this contact information:

- Ask to speak to the Advertising Officer, Executive or Director (or email them if an email address has been stated).

- Tell them that you are considering whether or not you would like to place an advert in their magazine or newspaper.

- Give them your dedicated email address and ask them to email you the advertising rates/ costs, readership numbers (i.e. how many people read/ purchase the publication). If the publication has fewer than 15, 000 – 20,000 readers, do not consider it. Likewise to advertising costs, ensure that adverts meet your dedicated budget at first and then you can expand as time goes on.

- Give them your PO Box address and ask them to send you at least three previous copies so that you can review what sort of adverts have been placed and whether you notice a frequency of certain adverts.

- Once you have reviewed the format and the type of adverts that are used in the newspaper(s) and magazine(s), write your own advert and do not forget to include your nominated website link(s) depending on what you are promoting.

- Remember the idea is to create interest and demand rather than trying to meet the demand that may be already saturated with existing competitors.

Chapter 9 – How much income can you make to pay for the wedding you *really* want?

You have come a long way and by completing all the tasks and by setting up various accounts and adverts, you have broken through the pain barrier. So the big question is, "After doing all of this, how much income can I make to pay for the wedding that I *really* want?"

The magic is in the numbers

In this book, a number of methods have been advised to demonstrate how you can set up a number of ways to generate income online.

The table below (Figure 1.1) shows an example of how creating multiple incomes streams on eBay makes a difference, in comparison to creating only one campaign.

I have used the example of the online eBay campaign that features on one of my websites www.mixedracehair.weebly.com .

The figures have been based on the eBay commission rates i.e.

- Up to £11* can be received for each person who registers on eBay so that they can purchase a product you are promoting and -

- Up to 60%* of each product that is sold can be received in commission.

(*Please note that these figures were correct at the time of researching).

Campaign:	Number of Google adverts directing to website:	Number of website campaigns running:	Daily marketing cost estimate:	Total Daily commission:	Daily profit made:
eBay in UK	1	1	50 clicks at £0.02 per click = £1.00 per advert. Total = £1	Out of 50 clicks only 1 person registered with eBay and purchased 1 item for £8.99. Totals £16.40	£16.40 - £1.00 = **£15.40 profit**
Based on existing example	5	5	100 clicks at £0.04 per click = £4 per advert. Total = £4 x 5 adverts = £20	Out of 100 clicks only 2 people registered with eBay and purchased 1 item each for £8.99. Totals £32.80 being made from each website	£32.80 x 5 website campaigns = £164. £164 - £20 in costs = **£144.00 profit**

Figure 1.1

In the first row, it shows an estimate of what I would make from 1 campaign that I used from my live example of eBay products (promoting mixed race hair products) based on the following eBay rates:

- £11 commission fee for registration (if the person does not have an eBay account and has to register).

- Up to 60% of purchasing a product in this instance the product costs £8.99 (the cheapest product available on my website) = approximately £5.40 gained in commission fees.

- Potential income that can be made daily equals £11 + £5.40 = £16.40.

- If you deduct the marketing costs for your Google adverts that equals £16.40 - £1.00 = £15.40 profit. If a person doesn't need to register on eBay then that equals £15.40 - £11.00 = £4.40 profit.

Based on the above figures, the table below (Figure 1.2) shows how much could potentially be made in 7 days/ 1 week:

Including new eBay registration:	Excluding eBay registration:
Possible daily profit = £15.40 x 7 days	Possible daily profit = £4.40 x 7 days
TOTAL: £107.80	TOTAL: £30.80

Figure 1.2

These examples of potential daily amounts of profit that can be made may seem unimpressive, however in the second row of Table/ Figure 1.1, it shows the potential profits if similar website campaigns were **duplicated** to promote other products.

For example, if 5 more eBay campaigns were created to feature on websites similar to the original campaign that promoted products, the potential profit that could be made increases:

- £22 commission for fee registration (assuming that your websites would attract more than 1 person due to more advertising and hyper links made to your other websites/ products and if the 2 people did not have an eBay account and they had to register).

- Up to 60% of purchasing the cheapest product listed on the website costing £8.99 per item = approximately £5.40 x 2 people = £10.80 gained in commission fees

- Potential income that can be made daily for each campaign equals £22.00 + £10.80 = £32.80.

- Multiply this potential daily amount for 5 campaigns running at the same time = £164.00.

- If you deduct the marketing costs for your 5 Google adverts (assuming that you would advertise more to drive more people to your dedicated websites and each click would cost you more to be in a high position on the first page of search results) that equals £164.00 - £20.00 = £144.00 in profit per day.

- If only 2 people per campaign visited your dedicated websites to purchase the cheapest product and they did not need to register with eBay because they have existing accounts, then profit would equal £144.00 - £110.00 (i.e. based on 2 people visiting your 5 website campaigns = 10 people x £11) = £34.00 in profit per day.

Based on the above figures, the table below (Figure 1.3) shows how much could potentially be made in 7 days/ 1 week:

Including new eBay registration:	Excluding eBay registration:
Possible daily profit = £144.00 x 7 days	Possible daily profit = £34.00 x 7 days
TOTAL: £1008.00	TOTAL: £238.00

Figure 1.3

Having 1 website campaign vs. having 5 website campaigns

Based on the above figures, the table below (Figure 1.4) shows how much could potentially be made in 7 days/ 1 week comparing having 1 website campaign to having 5:

	1 website campaign	5 website campaigns
Weekly profit including new eBay registration:	£107.80	£1008.00
Weekly profit excluding eBay registration:	£30.80	£238.00

Figure 1.4

So rather than making a weekly profit of £100.80 from 1 campaign, 5 campaigns could create a potential profit of £1008.00 based on my examples.

Even if only 2 of the cheapest products (in my example of purchasing a product for £8.99) were purchased and generated an income of £10.80 per day, in 1 week that is a total of £75.60 per week from 1 website. The point is - imagine if you created 10 more websites promoting products of a similar price or of a higher value?

Creating multiple income streams

Applying the same principle of creating more than a "one-off" campaign will soon create the opportunity for you to generate multiple income streams. If you duplicate the number of examples that have been demonstrated in this book, you are likely to meet your financial goal quicker to have the wedding that you *really* want.

This can be applied to creating more hoplinks to promote products from APP programmes like Clickbank or creating more reviews on your own websites as well as using Google Trends to assist you in creating more specific adverts to target your identified groups.

If you have not been aware of these possibilities, you now have an introductory knowledge of how to utilise the internet for activities other than checking your emails, paying bills and shopping online.

The sky is the limit and utilising the internet in this way can either supplement your current efforts to pay for the wedding that you *really* want or with discipline and determination, it is possible that these multiple incomes CAN pay for the wedding that you *really* want!

NOTE: Potential profits will vary from day to day, depending on what searchers are looking for on the internet. However, if you focus your time to create a number of campaigns, you will soon be able to delete those campaigns which are not making your desired income targets. Take note that marketing costs can vary for example a more popular advertising campaign may require you to pay a higher rate for each click made on one of your adverts; which has been considered on the above eBay example. The cost may be recouped if you are promoting a highly priced product or service.

The Challenge

Imagine if you applied the knowledge that you know now and created 20, 30 or even 100 campaigns? You could definitely meet your ultimate goal of being able to pay for the wedding that you *really* want. Albeit, be aware that it is likely that you would have to spend more if your adverts on Google attracted more clicks from searchers for example, but as you continue, you will find what works best for promoting your campaigns.

Remember that it is possible to choose a product or service you want to promote and to create a new campaign and website to promote your selected products/ services every day. After you read this book again:

- Challenge yourself to research products and services that you, your family and friends are either interested in or which do not have current or extensive promotion and create 1 campaign a week for 4 weeks.

- After 4 weeks, challenge yourself to identify and promote products twice a week for 2 weeks.

- After 2 weeks, challenge yourself to identify and promote at least 1 product and/ or service EVERY DAY!

You will have a range of online income streams in a relatively short period of time, **depending on your own work ethic and commitment** to meeting your financial goals.

Remember our couple – Rina and Kai back in Chapter 1...

If you can understand the method of duplication, you will soon find that the monthly (and daily) income targets you created alongside Rina and Kai *can* be met. If you review Rina and Kai's example, you can see that with the methods described in this book, their daily target of generating income totalling £47.90 for the next 6 months can be achieved.

Rina and Kai's Total income target for their wedding = £8618.61
Monthly Target Income = £8618.61 / by 6 (i.e. 6 months) = £1436.44
Daily Target Income = £1436.44/ by 30 (i.e. 30 days) = £47.90

Promoting products and offers

As you get more confident in promoting products and services, you will find that your own methods will become more sophisticated and earn you more income to meet the goal of having the wedding that you *really* want.

There are a couple of things that you may want to consider to support you with your progress:

TIP – Register the websites that you create with Google

You can register your websites with Google if you go to:

http://www.google.com/addurl/ . The page below will appear. Cut and paste or type in your website address and add it into the field marked as A below. Then complete the submission by typing in the required code before clicking the "Add URL" button.

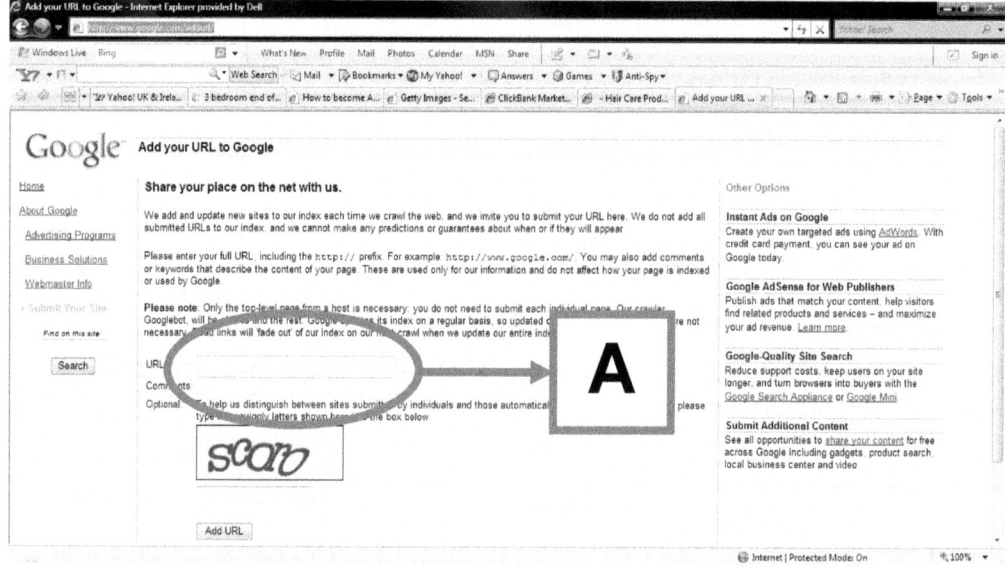

TIP - Promote offers that are already generating money

Sometimes, it is worth promoting products that are popular and then thinking creatively how the product or service can be promoted to a number of different customer profiles or audiences. You do not have to exert yourself and attempt to think of every possible customer profile, just ask yourself – "How can this product or service be relevantly promoted to another group?"

TIP - Promote offers that are "In Season"

There are some products that are likely to be searched for at more times than at others and related keywords will be used to search for these products or services. For example, "Valentine's day" related keywords are likely to generate a huge Google search word surge at the beginning of February. Or "Weight-loss" related keywords are likely to be used for searching heavily at the beginning of January. Being aware of standard seasons throughout the year (or the typical times for special occasions) can help you target your income generating activities with more relevance.

TIP - ONLY use keywords that are already PROVEN!

Anytime you are launching a new campaign, it is unwise to try and guess if a keyword(s) will work or not for your offer.

When you are generating sizable profits, you will be able to afford testing a wide range of keywords and new ideas for advertising.

Breakthroughs happen rarely – so always start out with keywords that others have (or are) already using to locate and promote products and services.

TIP – Review what already exists and improve it to make it better

There are possibly thousands of people who are promoting a number of different products and/ or services however you can search for products and services that you choose to promote to see how others are presenting and promoting products. Look at their websites and landing pages. Are they clear? Are there relevant images being used to support the content etc? Do not try to re-invent the wheel - view what is already working, make it better and then use it to take over and penetrate your chosen market(s) or customer profiles.

TIP – Check your Google Adwords account daily

Unless you use keywords that are actually used often enough to allow searchers the opportunity to view your adverts and related websites to promote products and services, you will find that you will be paying for keywords that are not effective.

It is important to monitor and keep track of the keywords that you use. Check and review your keywords that are recorded in your Google Adwords account. Google have an excellent system where it records the best performing keywords that are linked to your campaigns. If there are keywords that are not being effective, you can review the settings of the campaigns that this affects.

A suggestion for monitoring and tracking your campaigns

Once you decide that you want to create more than one campaign for each method described in this book, you need some way to keep a record of all the products and/ or services that you have created.

I have created a very simple document in Word Excel to assist you in your initial tracking so that you can view the number of products or campaigns that you promote and create. Hopefully this will prompt you to monitor and check your campaigns daily, until you find a more sophisticated way of doing this.

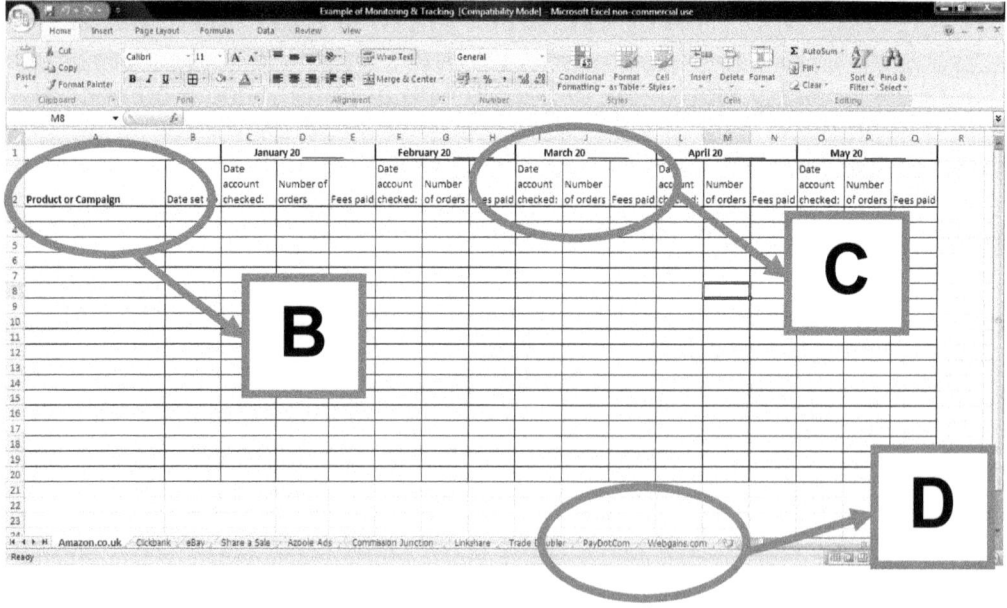

- In column A (marked as B) you can list the product or service that you are promoting on behalf of the company or affiliate programme that you have registered with. In this example, on the Amazon tab, I would list "Eminem Relapse Album" in relation to the example I have demonstrated in this book for you. In column B on the spreadsheet, you can note the date that you set up or started the campaign for your quick reference.

- In the row numbered as 1 on the spreadsheet, the month and year can be listed. Under each heading, 3 columns (marked as C) detail the date that you checked the account for your product(s) and/or campaigns, the number of orders received and the amount of commission or fees that have been generated and due to be paid to you.

- Using Word Excel can allow you to name each company that you are affiliated with on each tab (marked as D).

I hope that you find this helpful to assist you in the beginning of your journey to generating online income to pay for the wedding that you *really* want.

Last words

These introductory methods that have been shared with you are legitimate and real. So in short:

- TAKE ACTION!

- ANYTHING IS POSSIBLE, so stay motivated.

- If your first online income streams seem slow in generating income, keep reviewing and improving what you do. Don't give up!

- You CAN definitely have the Wedding that you *really* want.

This is just the beginning - all the best!

Wedding resources that you may find helpful for your special day

There are a wide range of resources available to help you have the wedding that you *really* want. Here are some suggestions:

Recommended shows, books, magazines and websites to inspire:

National Wedding Show - http://www.nationalweddingshow.co.uk/

WANG, Vera (2002) *Vera Wang on Weddings*, First Edition, HarperCollins

HAYWOOD, Sarah (2006) *Wedding Bible,* Illustrated Edition, The Wedding Bible Company Ltd

ANDERSON, Jane (2006), *A Place to Wed: Romantic and Exotic Wedding Destinations from Around the World*, Conran Octopus Ltd

County Wedding magazines - http://www.yourlondonweddingmagazine.co.uk/

Regional magazines can be viewed for inspiration for your perfect day.

Brides' Magazine - http://www.bridesmagazine.co.uk/

This magazine offers a 12 month planner, fashion advice, beauty tips, themes for your wedding and much more.

You and Your Wedding - http://www.youandyourwedding.co.uk/

This magazine offers a range of ideas and directory services for honeymoon destinations, wedding reception venues and case studies.

Confetti.co.uk - http://www.confetti.co.uk/

This online resource offers expert advice and directory services. Confetti also has retail stores that you can visit.

Wedding Pages - http://www.weddingpages.co.uk/

This online resource is a directory heaven to locate wedding suppliers.

About the Author

With a solid professional background in project and client management, spanning over 10 years, Denese L. Chikwendu has worked on managing the delivery of a number of campaigns, projects and programmes, specifically in Advertising & Communications and within Secondary School Education in the UK.

Denese's professional focus has earned her BA (Hons) and Master degrees in Design Management specialising in Corporate Communications and Business Management. She is also a PRINCE2 qualified Project Manager.

Denese transferred her experience to project-manage her own wedding in July 2008 which prompted her to take a closer look at what alternatives could be applied to help others to pay for the wedding they *really* want. Applying the principles of project management and budgeting soon made her realise that financing a wedding could easily escalate into a challenge that many couples may not be fully prepared for.

As a writer, entrepreneur and serial traveller, Denese aspires to offer support and encouragement to others. Alongside this, she has an ongoing involvement in project-managing campaigns and projects and continues to explore the value of Community Cohesion and Leadership. She believes that meeting the needs of local communities is a principle that aligns itself with the giving of your time, skills and resources. Denese aspires to continue to teach others alternatives so that they can make their personal contributions to others (and themselves) inspirational and full of impact. She is thirty years old.

Acknowledgments

First of all, thank you Heavenly Father for being loving and faithful. You are the Alpha and Omega, the Beginning and the End.

To my husband Ifeanyi, thank you for being a kind, supportive and loving husband. You are awesome my sweetheart. You are a man of strength, courage and vision. Thank you for always encouraging me to chase after my dreams. Thank you for always listening and thank you for cheering me on when nobody else is around. You delight me.

To my Granny, Edna Anderson, I love you. Thank you for being a wise and wonderful mother to me. May you always have grace and favour.

Thank you to all of my best friends - you definitely know who you are. Thank you for your friendships which have caused you to become my inner circle, my family. Your ongoing, support and encouragement has been invaluable to me.

Finally, Daddy, I love you. Mum, I miss you. I wish you could see how much I have done so far.

www.ingramcontent.com/pod-product-compliance
Ingram Content Group UK Ltd.
Pitfield, Milton Keynes, MK11 3LW, UK
UKHW051255180426
11947UKWH00020B/1720